THE
EASTERN
EUROPE
COLLECTION

TRAVELS THROUGH GERMANY, RUSSIA, AND POLAND IN THE YEARS 1769 AND 1770

Joseph Marshall

ARNO PRESS & THE NEW YORK TIMES

New York - 1971

12 2158

Reprint Edition 1971 by Arno Press Inc.

Reprinted from a copy in
The Columbia University Library

LC# 77-135821

ISBN 0-405-02763-X

The Eastern Europe Collection
ISBN for complete set: 0-405-02730-3

Manufactured in the United States of America

Publisher's Note: Travels through Germany,
Russia, and Poland in the years 1769 and 1770
was the only section reprinted from the original
two volume edition of Travels through Holland, Flanders, Germany, Denmark, Sweden,
Lapland, Russia, The Ukraine, and Poland in
the years 1768, 1769, and 1770.

TRAVELS

THROUGH

HOLLAND,	LAPLAND,
FLANDERS,	RUSSIA,
GERMANY,	The UKRAINE,
DENMARK,	AND
SWEDEN,	POLAND,

IN THE

Years 1768, 1769, and 1770.

In which is particularly Minuted,

THE PRESENT STATE

OF

THOSE COUNTRIES,

RESPECTING THEIR

AGRICULTURE, POPULATION,

MANUFACTURES, COMMERCE,

THE ARTS, AND USEFUL UNDERTAKINGS.

By JOSEPH MARSHALL, Esq;

VOL. III.

LONDON:

Printed for J. ALMON, opposite Burlington House, Piccadilly.

MDCCLXXII.

CONTENTS of VOL. III.

Travels through Ruffia.

CONTENTS.

Travels

Travels through Russia.

CHAP. IV.

Defcription of Peterfburg—General Accounts of the Empire of Ruffia—The Emprefs— Government—Manufactures—Trade—Army —Navy—Prefent State.

I Arrived at Peterfburg the evening of the 24th. and, as I defigned making fome ftay in the city, determined to hire private lodgings; for I had been informed that the publick inns were not only very extravagant, but alfo very bad, which indeed is the cafe in all capitals, for, where the people of quality do not go, (having houfes of their own) one is always fure of meeting with very indifferent treatment. I hired a firft floor, confifting, after the Ruffian fafhion, of two dining-rooms, a drawing-room, dreffing-room, and bed-chamber, befides fervants' apartments, for three guineas a week; fuch a fuit of rooms as at London it would be very difficult to have at twelve. Peterfburg is built on feveral iflands, which were once nothing more than marfhy fpots of mud over-run with reeds: but the immortal Peter, whofe undertakings in every thing carried a magnificence of idea in them that can never be fufficiently admired, converted a miferable bog into a fine city.

4 And

And here I cannot avoid anfwering the re-flections of feveral writers againft that immortal monarch, for facrificing more than half a million of men in founding this city. The Czar's object was to become an European Power, which without a port on the Baltick he might as well have pretended to be an American one. His vaft dominions, though contiguous to Poland, and themfelves a part of Europe, were at fuch a diftance from the European theatre, and in fo barbarous a ftate, that nothing but opening himfelf a way to the Baltick could poffibly bring his grand plan to bear. By founding this city, and making it the capital of his empire, and a fea-port fit to receive the naval force he deftined to act on that fea, he anfwered all his purpofes at one ftroke; and confequently could fcarcely pay too dearly for the propofed advantage. As to the lofs of fuch numbers of lives, the fault certainly was not fo much owing to the fteadinefs of the Czar's adhering to his plan, as to not taking proper care of the men while they were at the work, fince every one muft be very fenfible that works, to the full as great as any he executed, could now be performed in England under fimilar circumftances, comparatively fpeaking, without the lofs of a man. But the confequences, which
we

we all know have flowed from the founding
this city, have been of such infinite importance to the Ruffian empire, that no expence
that could ever have been incurred would have
been too great for gaining such fignal benefits. Peterfburg is the foul of commerce
in all thefe Northern parts; it is the foundation on which all the Ruffian naval force has
been erected; and the port, on which moft
depends their nurfery of failors. At the fame
time that thefe capital circumftances attend
it, it muft be acknowledged that it is very deficient as a receptacle of the men of war of a
great empire; for the depth of water, the frefh-
nefs of it, the docks, yards, every thing at Peterfburg, are againft the ufe of it for that purpofe. The yards are at Petersburg, but the
depth of water is fo inconfiderable that nothing can be put aboard the firft-rate men of
war before they are conveyed to Cronflot,
which is not eafily done neither. Once this
work was effected by means of moft expenfive machines, but now they come without
that difficulty by means of the new canal,
which is not however fo complete but that
infinite attention is neceffary for conducting
them. It is not only men of war, however,
that are built in thefe yards : galleys * are
much

* Count Algarotti, mentioning the naval power of the
Ruffians,

much in ufe for the Baltick; but, as this empire has experienced of late great changes, in
the

Ruffians, obferves, " Galleys are here the proper things.
Be there never fo little water, there is always enough for
them.   They glide between the little iflands and the
rocks ; they can land any where.   The Czar was fenfible of it at laft, and fent for galley-builders from Ve-
nice.   I met with one of them greatly advanced in years,
and was not a little furprifed to hear terminations in *ao* in
fixty degrees of latitude.   The galleys that one fees here
are of different fizes ; there are fmall ones, which carry
about one hundred and thirty men, and others much
larger.   They are all armed with two pieces of cannon
on the prow, and furnifhed with chace-guns and fwivels
on the fides.   The Czar gave to each of them the name
of a Ruffian fifh.   Now they are numbered as the legions
were ; there are upwards of one hundred and thirty of
them, and they are to be much more numerous.   By this
means an army of thirty thoufand men is tranfported with
great eafe.   Rowing is to the Ruffian foldiers what the
exercife of fwimming was to the Romans. Every foot-fol-
dier learns to handle the oar at the fame time as the mufket,
by which means, without maritime commerce, and without embargoes, the Ruffians have always crews ready for
their galleys.   They caft anchor every night, and land
where it is leaft expected.   When difembarked, they
draw them up upon the land, range them in a circle
with their prows and artillery pointed outward, and thus
they have in a trice a fortified camp.   They leave five or
fix battalions to guard it, and with the reft of their troops
over-run the country, and lay it under contribution.
The expedition ended, they re-embark, and begin again
in another quarter.   Sometimes they tranfport their veffels
from one water to another over a flip of land, as was
practifed by the antients on feveral occafions, and particularly

the fyftem of politicks, the ufe of galleys vary.
In a war on the coaft of the Baltick they are
increafed in number; but, when a peace
comes, they are neglected, and not kept up
indeed in the manner they ought to be. During the late war, they might have annoyed
the Pruffian dominions infinitely more than
they did; but the great army was the only
thing attended to.

Peterfburg is amazingly increafed in fize
within thefe forty years: At the death of
Peter the Great, it did not contain eighty
thoufand

cularly after the example of Mahomet II. at the fiege of
Conftantinople.

" The Swedes can teftify whether thefe Ruffian galleys
are formidable. They have feen them ravage their rich
mines of Norkopping, the whole coafts of Gothland and
Sudermania, and fhew themfelves even before Stock-
holm."——He alfo adds another circumftance, which is
worthy of note, concerning the timber ufed for fhip-
building here.———" Of what wood do you think the
fhips are built at Peterfburg ? It is a fpecies of oak which
is at leaft two fummers upon the road before it arrives. It
comes ready cut by the carpenter from the kingdom of
Cafan. It goes a little way up the Wolga, then the
Tuertza, paffes through a canal into the fea, from thence
into the Mefta, and by means of the Volcova falls into a
canal which conveys it into the lake Ladoga, from
thence it defcends at laft by the Neva to Peterfburg. I
faw in this port a floop built at Cafan, from whence it
came by the rivers I have juft mentioned, which join the
Cafpian fea to the Baltick, and are a quite different thing
from the famous canal of Languedock."

thoufand inhabitants, and now the Ruffians affert that there are five hundred thoufand, but this is an exaggeration. It covers a very great extent of land and water; the ftreets are fome of them very broad, long, and with canals in the middle of them; and others are planted in the Dutch fafhion, which I before obferved is a wretched plan; the houfes are immenfely large : the palaces of the nobility, I think exceed in fize thofe of any city I have feen; and that of the Emprefs is an amazing ftructure; but let me remark that they are rather great than beautiful : the fize is all that ftrikes you : and thefe prodigious piles are ftuck fo thick with ornaments, that there is hardly any fuch thing as judging of their proportions : the Italian architecture is mixed with the Dutch, and the whole forms very inelegant buildings, in which true tafte is totally facrificed to a profufion of ornament. But if the eye does not fcrutinize into the feparate parts of the buildings, but takes only the ftreets at large, the city may be fairly pronounced a very fine one.

The Czar himfelf fpared no pains in rendering it as ftrong as poffible; for being at the very extremity of his dominions, clofe to his enemies the Swedes, and open to the attacks which were poffible to arife from his European connections,

connections, he made a point of having it impregnable; but herein he certainly failed. There are many forts and whole shores converted into platforms, and lined from end to end with great guns. These works begin at Cronflot, which is made very strong, and they laft to the city. There is a citadel regularly built, and capable not only of protecting the city on one fide, but also itfelf of standing a fiege. Yet there are many feamen who affert that a fleet of ships well manned and conducted, and provided with a proper number of firefhips, and bomb-ketches, would without any great difficulty lay all Peterfburg in ashes. I muft own myfelf of a very different opinion, for here is always a very confiderable fleet of men of war, from 60 to 100 guns, with numerous failors, that could man them on a very fhort notice; thefe fhips properly difpofed by way of batteries, would render fuch an attempt impracticable, even if the fortifications are granted to be deficient, which is more than will be allowed by many officers well skilled in this part of their art.

Among the publick buildings, there are many extremely worthy the attention of a traveller, particularly the dock yards and naval magazines, the arfenal, foundery, admiralty, &c. without infifting on the imperial palace,

the

the cathedral, or many churches. In the
docks they have a great number of carpenters
continually at work, among whom are many
Englifh, difcharged by the government on
the conclufion of the peace in 1763, they
meet with great encouragement here, and are
much better employed than if in the fervice
of France or Spain. They build here all forts
of veffels, from fhips of one hundred and
twenty guns, (and fome much larger have
been known) down to boats, and the number
always on the ftocks at a time is confiderable.
After the death of Peter the Great the marine
was neglected, infomuch, that the Emprefs's
naval ftrength was not computed to be a fifth
part of what that great monarch poffeffed, and
this was owing to a want of trade, which
can alone make feamen; unlefs when in the
hands of fuch a man as Peter, who created
every thing: But the prefent Emprefs, who
has thrown the fpirit of that great monarch
into all the departments of the ftate, has re-
vived it wonderfully, fo that at prefent the
Ruffians have a formidable navy, and in a
few years will have a yet more confiderable
one.

There is fcarcely any thing at Peterfburg
more deferving notice than the foundery:
The iron is brought from Kexholm by water,
and

and the number of cannon and mortars that are caſt here is very great; alſo cannon balls, ſhells, and all ſorts of military implements in which iron is uſed; which are made here at as ſmall an expence as in Sweden, or any other part of the world. The arſenal is always well ſtored with them; and there are vaſt q uantities made on a private account for exportation, forming a very conſiderable branch of commerce.

The trade of Peterſburg is much more conſiderable than that of any other town in the Ruſſian empire; and would figure on compariſon with many very great marts in other parts of Europe, but unfortunately that vaſt commerce is nine-tenths of it carried on in foreign bottoms. The Dutch alone load annually here with timber, iron, and all ſorts of naval ſtores a great many ſhips, and the Engliſh many more.

The commodities theſe nations carry from Petersburg are tar, bees wax, pitch, hemp, flax, leather, ſkins, furs, pot-aſhes, timber, plank, iron, yarn, linen, lintſeed &c. and theſe in ſuch quantities that the very ballance of trade between Great-Britain and Ruſſia has been reckoned at four hundred thouſand pounds a year againſt the former; the amount of the total commerce may therefore be eaſily conceived. The royal navy of Eng-

land is almoft totally fupplied with hemp
from Petersburg, great quantities of iron, and
other naval ftores, and all the fhipping in England likewife; and this importation has increafed very much fince the Swedes laid a prohibi-
tion on our manufactures, fo that the importation from that country was reduced to the few
articles which neceffity obliged us to have from
thence; and all the reft very politically trans-
ferred to Ruffia.

The great amount of the commerce between us and this empire has been the occafion of very many political differtations and
treatifes proving the neceffity of encouraging
the production of all the commodities we import from Ruffia, in our colonies; and I
think our politicians have not in any inftance
had better grounds for their opinions, or fupported their propofitions with more unanfwerable arguments. A trading nation fhould never
regret parting with its money when fhe
thereby adds to her induftry; but in this cafe
we pay three or four hundred thoufand
pounds a year to Ruffia for thofe commodities which our own colonies would produce;
and the difference is that now we pay in
cafh, but to our colonies we fhould pay in
manufactures: confequently, for want of
this meafure being effected, we lofe the employment

ployment of so many of our poor as could earn the whole amount of that sum; and we also lose the general profit resulting to the nation at large by their earning such a sum of money; for any increase of our national income raised by an increase of industry, is beneficial to us in a much greater degree than the mere amount of it. To illustrate this, let us consider the advantage to Russia of our paying her a ballance of three or four hundered thousand pounds. That ballance is paid to a certain number of merchants and dealers at Petersburg and other ports; they pay it to a set of landlords, miners, husbandmen, and manufacturers. These again pay it to all the manufacturers, tradesmen, &c. with whom they deal; and these to a fresh set. Now every art, trade, business, and profession in the whole empire come in for an additional income from this sum circulating through the mass of industry; and every one of them are essentially the richer. If this circulation could be traced, it would probably be found, that three hundred thousand pounds a year gained in the precious metal, were equal in general improvement to the value of nine or twelve hundred thousand pounds a year. Because no one can be supposed to have an increase of income in Russia,

I 2   any

any more than any where elfe, without increafing his expences proportionably ; that is,
he buys more food, more cloth, more fhoes,
employs more builders, and, in a word,
more artifts of all forts.   None of which can
increafe without reciprocal benefits flowing
back again; and the government from the
whole circulation in every ftep it takes feizes
a part by means of taxes.   This is but a
flight fketch of the effects of an increafing
wealth ; to explain it fully would take a much
greater compafs.

The greateft trade at Petersburg is carried
on by the Englifh ; next in rank come the
Dutch ; as to the French, they deal here as
little as poffible ; for the two crowns are very
far from being on a good footing, the French
and the Swedes being in clofe alliance, they
therefore trade to Sweden for all thofe commodities which England gets from Ruffia,
fome few excepted, which are not to be had
at that market.   Notwithftanding this, they
confume large quantities of French commodities in Ruffia, but thefe come to them
principally through the hands of the Dutch.

The building this capital has had a very
great effect in improving large tracks of
land in the furrounding provinces : The corn
and other provifions which are brought hither,

ther, and the variety of merchandize that is exported from hence, employ fome of the moft confiderable inland navigations in the world. The Neva, the great lakes of Lagoda and Onega; the Tuerka, the Mefta, the Volcova and the Wolga, all thefe rivers, with many others, tho' fome of them are at a great diftance, keep open a communication between Petersburg and thofe noble tracks of country upon the Cafpian and Euxine feas : but it may be fuppofed that the greateft advantages are made by the people who have not fuch a diftance to go ; fo that the products of all the neighbouring provinces are infinitely greater that thofe of others more diftant.

I have heard fome Ruffians affirm, that all this feeming increafe of culture, of manufactures, and of commerce, is imaginary, that it is all owing to the fovereign's fixing the feat of government here, which has not raifed a new population, but drawn an old one from other provinces. Mofcow was once the metropolis, and the feat of government, &c. and Novogorod the great ftaple of trade, but Petersburg now is both ; and has half depopulated thofe cities, as well as Archangel, which was once a place of very great trade. In anfwer to this I allow, that part of the affertion is true ; that much of the population

I 3   of

of this city, and its neighbourhood, is owing
to a defertion of other places ; but at the fame
time I muft infift, that a new population muft
have been created by means of this city, becaufe a new induftry has fprung up, new
trades opened, new manufactures eftablifhed,
and innumerable artifts employed, which were
not in being before ; and many of which
could not have been in being had not this city
been founded. There is no doubt, but the
Ruffian commodities found, in fmall quantities, their way into Europe before Peter the
Great's time ; but every one muft be fenfible
of the comparative fmallnefs of the quantity
when they had not an European port, and
when all their products, in order to get to the
Baltick, were forced to fubmit to a long land
carriage through an enemy's country, and
fubject to whatever duties that enemy chofe
to lay on them. The prefent method of carrying on their trade, manufactures and products has I think every advantage over the
former ; and if this is allowed, it follows
of courfe, that population is proportionably
increafed, and wealth moft certainly ; both
which have a direct effect in raifing the value of land for a great diftance around the
capital.

But the building of the city was a work of
the

the Great Peter's, which is giving it all the illuſtration that is neceſſary; for if ever mortal was endowed with the true art of governing, with that kind of univerſal ge- nius equally great in practice and ſpecula- tion, it was him. All his ideas, all his plans had ſomething ſo great and compre- henſive in them; ſuch a power of foreſeeing future events, and ſuch abilities in providing for them, that he never once failed in theory, tho' in practice obſtacles ſometimes aroſe which were beyond his power to counteract. The founding of Peterſburg is one capital inſtance; for ever ſince he made it the ſeat of his ma- rine, and the principal trading town of his dominions, it has been of more real ſervice to the empire than any other meaſure he could poſſibly have adopted. What an extent of political imagination is diſplayed in his inland navigations! They have a greatneſs unrival- led in any other part of the world. But the moſt capital project of the Czar's was that wherein he planned a navigation to the Medi- terranean.—Next to Petersburg the favourite of his empire was Azoph, the reaſon of which was his deſign of eſtabliſhing a trade from thence thro' the Thracian Boſphorus to the Archipe- lago. This would not only have given him greater mercantile advantages than Petersburg,

I 4   but

but would have endangered the very being
of the Turkish empire; by letting a naval
power of the Ruffians into the very heart of
Conftantinople; and that Peter defigned fomething more than commerce, we may eafily
gather from his forming docks, yards, and
naval magazines, at Azoph; and actually
had fhips of feventy guns upon the ftocks,
which fufficiently fhewed that he intended
a naval war upon the Euxine fea againft the
Turks.

The Ruffian empire, though of fuch an
amazing extent, is very well known to be
badly peopled. The beft writers inform us,
that it contains feventeen millions of inhabitants, and one million in the conquered provinces; but from the beft accounts I could get
at Petersburg, I believe the number at prefent
to be more confiderable. Almoft from the
moment that the prefent emprefs began to
reign, fhe has increafed the number of her
fubjects by many ways, principally by a general and very active encouragement of all arts,
of agriculture, mining, manufactures and commerce, and this with fuch effect, that all of
them are more nourifhing at this time by many
degrees than they were twenty years ago.
And another means which fhe has taken to increafe her people has been inviting foreigners;
this

this she has done in a still greater degree than any of her predecessors ; almost from her accession to the empire she has brought continual bodies of Germans, Poles, and Greeks from Turkey, to settle in her dominions, and these not few in numbers; from the coasts of Germany ship loads, but from Poland and Turkey whole towns, villages and districts have left their habitations and settled in Russia; nor has it been only at certain times, but regular emigration in consequence of her continued encouragement.

This encouragement which the Empress has constantly granted consists in several very important articles. All the expences of the journey, or voyage from their native country, are borne by her ; she feeds and supports them by the way. Upon their arrival at the territory appointed them to cultivate (which has always been part of the crown lands) every family has a cottage erected at her expence, to which they contribute labour ; they then are furnished with implements necessary for cultivation, and one year's provisions for the whole family. A further advantage is an exemption from all taxes during five years. All which is a system of such admirable policy, and carried into execution with such unusual spirit, even while the finances of the empire have

been

been much diftreffed by expenfive wars, that I know not an inftance in hiftory fuperior to it. There can be no doubt but the advantages muft be immenfe, not only in population, but alfo revenue; for thefe fettlers, though they have an affignment of lands for ever, yet it is, after a certain number of years, under payment of an annual quit-rent, fufficient to produce a confiderable revenue. The continued diforders in Poland, and the oppreffions in Turkey, have caufed many thoufands of families annually to leave their country, and make ufe of this bounty of the emprefs. By this time the increafe of people muft be very great; fome perfons, whofe information I believe is very good, affured me, that the number of fouls thus gained, fince the acceffion of the prefent Czarina, is not lefs than fix hundred thoufand; I muft own the number appears almoft incredible. We may, without fuppofing the total fo very great, eafily fee from hence that fhe muft have raifed the revenue of the crown lands very much, and put them in a way of being yet more improved; for certainly peopling them was the firft rational ftep that could be taken, and one which never could deceive her. I made enquiries concerning the fituation of the emigrants, and whether all the promifes that

had

had been made to them had been executed, and I was affured that they were moſt punctually ; but that in very many caſes much more was done for them than promiſed, and every effort taken to make them perfectly ſatisfied with their choice ; a proof of which is the increaſed numbers that have been coming from the beginning: the accounts ſent back by the firſt ſettlers, being ſuch as induced others to take the ſame meaſures, and this effect has been regular ever ſince, ſo that the number of new comers is at preſent greater than ever, and promiſes to be ſo conſiderable, that in a few years, if the troubles in Poland continue, the increaſe of people here will be immenſe, and with them certainly that of the power, and wealth of the empire. Nor has any event of her reign diſcovered a greater underſtanding than this regular favour ſhewn to population.

The revenues of the Ruſſian empire are very great, conſidering the value of money; which in theſe ſort of diſquiſitions ought ever to be conſidered, though it rarely is ſo. The Empreſs is in many articles the ſole merchant in her dominions. The whole trade by land to China is on her account : this is not indeed conſiderable, for a carravan rarely goes now. Rhubarb, pot-aſhes, and ſpices, are branches in which ſhe, and no body elſe, trades.

4

trades. Salt is an article that brings her in an immenfe revenue. Very large quantities of the beft hemp of the Ukrain are bought and fold on her account; much iron, the fame; and even beer and brandy are her's. Befides thefe articles, fhe has cuftoms, tolls, and a poll-tax of three fhillings and fix-pence a head. The crown-lands, which are prodigioufly extenfive, bring in a confiderable revenue.

The following general account was fhewn me at Petersburg of the Emprefs's revenue, reckoned in Englifh money. It is handed about there, and thought to be not very far from the truth in any article.

Poll-tax	1,750,000
Crown-lands	672,000
Salt	542,000
Hemp and iron	370,000
China trade Rhubarb and Spices -	48,000
Pot-afhes	60,000
Cuftans	179,000
Baths and licenfed houfes	68,000
Other duties &c. comprehending all other taxes	400,000
Total	£ 4,089,000

But the value of fuch a revenue will not appear

appear clearly to any reader, that does not confider the great difference of the value of money in this country, and others that are full of commerce and wealth; upon the neareft computation I can make, thefe four millions are about as good as ten in England. And if we fuppofe them ten, we fhall then fee the great importance of liberty, trade and manufactures in raifing a publick revenue; for eighteen or nineteen millions of people in Ruffia, yield no greater revenue than a third of that number yield in England. Wealth therefore depends no further on population than the induftry of that population extends. It is a flourifhing agriculture, improving manufactures, and an extenfive commerce which yield a great publick revenue. Introducing induftry among all claffes of people that were not induftrious before, is therefore as effential an increafe of inhabitants as bringing in foreign emigrants: both thefe means have been employed by the prefent fovereign of Ruffia, for the aggregate of the induftry of this empire is vaftly more confiderable than when fhe came to the throne.

She has iffued out feveral edicts for the encouragement of agriculture; and herein fhe has proceeded with her ufual politicks; for fhe rightly confidered that the way to make this

moft

moſt uſeful of all the arts to flouriſh is to ſet its profeſſors at eaſe; ſhe has accordingly given a much greater degree of liberty to the peaſants than ever they enjoyed before; for they were greater ſlaves than even in Poland; but now every nobleman (called yet Boyards in Ruſſia) whoſe eſtate conſiſts of a given number of families, is obliged to enfranchiſe one family every year, and they are directed by the Empreſs to ſelect for this purpoſe the moſt induſtrious family they have: the peaſant has a farm aſſigned him, and the Empreſs makes him a preſent of ſome implement of the greateſt uſe; but he is by the ſame edict to pay after three years a rent to the nobleman that is very conſiderable; the deſign of which is to convince the nobility of the advantage of letting their eſtates to the peaſants to be paid a rent in money: and I was informed that many of them had made a great progreſs in it, partly from conviction of its expediency, and partly from paying their court to the ſovereign.

Beſides this meaſure, there are great encouragements given both in freedom, and in exemption from taxes and ſervices, to all thoſe who improve waſte lands, by bringing them into culture. Such a ſyſtem is highly neceſſary in an empire that contains more land than Europe, but not more inhabitants than Germany;

Germany; and where immenfe tracks of as fine foil as any in the world are utterly wafte. If the life of the prefent Emprefs is a long one, great things will be done in this walk of improvement, and many very extenfive territories cultivated which have hitherto laid wafte. The foreigners which fhe has fettled, and continues to fettle, and the encouragement which hufbandry meets with, will have a great effect in giving a new countenance to the agriculture of many provinces.

I made enquiries concerning the prefent ftate of Ruffian manufactures, and was informed that they have never been able to make them any thing confiderable: They have at Peterfburg fome very large founderies, where all forts of ammunition and military ftores are made; and they make fome very good cloth of hemp, but the quantity of this laft is not confiderable. There are many other fabricks, but not of confequence, nor any ways proportioned to the number of the people. They have many woollen manufactories, but they do not cloath even their own army. England has the greateft fhare in the commerce of fupplying them; the import at Peterfburg of coarfe and fine woollen cloths is very confiderable: what we do not fend them, they have from the Dutch; but the French

fend

fend none. Nor is there hardly a manufactory in England that does not fend great quantities of its fabricks hither; and notwithftanding fo great an exportation, yet the importation of hemp, iron, &c. is fo great, that a large ballance is paid (as I before mentioned) to Ruffia. There are feveral inftances of much encouragement being given to the national manufactures, but the effect has not been great, and I muft own myfelf of opinion that it never will be great, for the Ruffian do not feem to take to any fort but thofe in which they are from their infancy converfant. They make excellent carpenters, fhip-builders, fmiths, and founders, but they will never make a figure as weavers.

It alfo deferves enquiry, whether it would be highly political to make any great efforts in complicated manufactures which require very many hands, while there is fo immenfe a territory to cultivate, and not of barren mountains like Sweden, but of great extended plains of as rich land, as the beft parts of England, or even Holland : confequently with fuch materials to work upon, it is much to be queftioned if a given number of hands would not in raifing hemp and flax, or making potafhes, bring in a greater fum of money to the country, than if they were employed in manufactures.

5

nufactures. It appears to me very clearly that they would. From the defcriptions which I have had of feveral immenfe provinces of this empire, I have no doubt but a thoufand pounds and ten people would, employed in attending cattle, yield a greater return in hides and tallow alone; than from any manufactures they could be employed in; for there are meadows (not bogs or marfhes) covered with fine grafs of an hundred fquare miles in a place, with no other inhabitants than what are wild, and very few of them. In a country where there is fuch plenty of excellent land, and through which run fo many navigable rivers that would convey all its products to a ready market; and notwithftanding thefe advantages, there are large waftes ftill on the very banks of thofe rivers—under fuch circumftances I apprehend, that no attention to manufactures can yield a profit equal to a proper cultivation : the wealth arifing from it would be far greater, the publick revenue would be much more improved, and population increafed in a much greater proportion. If I was fufficiently verfed in the theory of ftocking ground with inftruments of tillage, and with cattle, &c. I fhould be able to make this appear by minute calculations; but I do not apprehend that there is any reaſon in general to doubt it.

While this is the caſe, whoever fills the throne of Ruſſia will moſt advance the intereſts of that empire by promoting, by every poſſible means the cultivation of ſo immenſe a territory; if there happens a ſuccſſieon for a long period of time of ſuch ſovereigns as at preſent fill that throne; this vaſt empire will be raiſed by theſe means to a pitch of grandeur, much exceeding what it at preſent poſſeſſes: and from the conduct which has been hitherto purſued by the preſent Empreſs, there is great reaſon to think that ſhe is ſenſible of the importance of directing her views principally to this end; they have hitherto been attended with ſuch ſucceſs, as to be a very ſtrong proof that the plan upon which ſhe has proceeded, is a juſt one; a different one might have been followed more in favour of manufactures, by planting the foreign emigrants thickly in the near neighbourhood of thoſe places only which have fabricks in them; with a view to the employment of many of them in theſe manufactures.

Relative to the commerce of Ruſſia, it ſhould be remembered previouſly to any enquiry into its preſent ſtate, that this immenſe empire is by no means ſituated advantageouſly for

for trade. The only ports that it poſſeſſes, from which any trade of conſequence can be carried on, are in the Baltick, a ſea that is frozen almoſt half the year; and, at the ſame time, it is at the extremity of the empire; ſo that the commodities, which are exported through this ſea, are obliged to be brought ſome thouſands of miles before they are put on board the ſhips. This is ſuch a diſadvantage, that it much affects the commerce of the empire, and is of a nature that will not admit of any remedy. This circumſtance conſidered, the commerce of Ruſſia is very conſiderable, as to the export of its products and commodities, but the ſhipping of the empire is very trifling compared with that to which ſhe gives employment. All the trade which the Engliſh carry on with Ruſſia is in their own bottoms; it is the ſame with the Dutch, and almoſt all other European nations; ſo that the Ruſſian flag is ſcarcely known in the world, although Ruſſian commodities are met with in ſo many places.

To remedy this evil by a general extenſion of commerce, and by procuring a navigation on a more favourable ſea, the Czar Peter the Great formed the noble plan of raiſing a naval power on the Black ſea, and eſtabliſhing a commerce on it, with a communication thro'

K 2 the

the fea of Conftantinople with the Mediterranean ; one of the greateft defigns which
could have entered the head of any fovereign
of Ruffia, and which would give a very confiderable fhare of the commerce of the world to
that empire. It fhould be remembered, that
the richeft products which Ruffia exports are
thofe of the moft fouthernly provinces, particularly the Ukraine ; which is univerfally
allowed to be one of the fineft countries in the
world ; the rivers which flow through this territory all take their courfe to the Black fea ;
fo that it is only by an artificial navigation,
and a long land carriage that they are brought
to Peterfburg. It is well known that they
could be delivered at Conftantinople for a
much lefs price than at Petersburg ; which,
with the increafe of trade refulting from a navigation open all the year, and immediately
into the center of Europe, would give the
empire at one ftroke, ten times the commerce
it can ever poffefs otherwife ; and would, at
the fame time, give the Czarina fuch an advantage over the Turks, as to endanger the very
exiftence of Conftantinople, and with it that
of their empire. And if the plan upon which
that great monarch conducted his wars againft
the Turks be confidered, it will appear that
he never loft fight of this great object. Azoph

was

was the town which he acquired at a very great expence of men and money : he fortified it at a yet greater expence, and built a fleet of ftout fhips for that navigation, with docks, yards, and magazines of all forts ; but the unfortunate campaign of the Pruth put an end to his hopes, and gave back that conqueft to the Turks. Had he been fuccefsful, he defigned the conqueft of the Crimea, which would at once have given him poffeffion of a noble province, and the command of the Euxine. The fame idea was fteadily purfued in the war of 1735, which ended with the ceffion of Azoph to the Ruffians, a fortrefs of all others the moft important for the profecution of this defign.

A very little reflection will give us an idea of fome of the confequences which would, in all probability, attend the execution of this plan. Without fuppofing an entire conqueft of Moldavia, Bulgaria, and Walachia, with the Tartar diftricts to the North of the fea, as fome writers have done, let us only ftate the navigation from the Euxine to the Mediterranean being made free to both nations, and Azoph and the Crimea in the hands of the Ruffians. They would then have a free navigation from all parts of their empire, by

means

means of the Tanais and the Donetz, down to Azoph; that port would then be the grand magazine of all the commodities of their empire, where their fhips would load for diftributing them through all the fouthern countries of Europe, and on the coaft of Africa, at the fame time that Petersburg fent them to all the Northern ones. But this trade would give them a new export, which would prove perhaps of more confequence than all the others put together; that of corn : the fineft territories of Europe for husbandry are faid to be the tracks on the North of the Black fea, including their province of the Ukraine; at prefent thefe countries have no vent for fuch a product, and therefore raife no more than for their own confumption; but, in cafe of fuch a Ruffian navigation as I am now fpeaking of, this teritorry would lie much better for fupplying the beft corn markets in Europe, than thofe which at prefent fupply them. Barbary and Sicily it is true yield an uncertain fupply; but it is well known that Holland fupplies moft of the demands of Portugal, Spain and Italy, when embargoes are laid in England; and the Dutch bring the corn they thus trade in from Dantzick; let the reader therefore compare the navigation from Azoph, to all the coafts of the Mediterranean, with that

5

from

from Dantzick, round three fourths of Europe. It is very evident, that the Ruffians would at once command the entire fupply of all thofe countries; not only with fo important an article as that of corn, but would, for the fame reafon, gain the exclufive trade of naval ftores to them likewife; iron, hemp, canvafs, timber, &c.

Relative to ftrength in war, the fuccefs of fuch a plan would only be too great; for one can hardly fuppofe the Turks would fubmit to a Ruffian navigation through the heart of Conftantinople, without they were firft reduced to the laft extremity; and in fuch a ftate of weaknefs their fubmitting to it would, in cafe of a fucceeding war, be but another word for the overthrow of their empire. It would depend on the naval force of the two empires on the Black fea, for which-ever fleet in cafe of a quarrel, was fuperior, they would nearly command the event of the war; if the Turks had the better, the Ruffians would be cut off from all the advantages propofed; and if victory declared for the latter, Conftantinople and all the provinces of the Ottoman empire would be expofed to them in the moft dangerous manner; and if the advantages of the Ruffians, in building and equipping fleets, with their territory behind them fo abounding with

K 4 all

all forts of materials, be confidered, it can hardly be doubted but they would gain the moft decifive fuperiority. Nor fhould I omit obferving, that the mere poffeffion of Azoph might be made a means of putting this plan in execution and carrying any future war, if well directed, to the gates of Conftantinople.

Let any one confider the prefent afpect of affairs in that quarter, and the motions of the Ruffian troops, and it will be evident that this idea is now in being, and that, in all probability, before the prefent war fees a period, the Turks will find the arms of Ruffia infinitely heavier than in the laft, and themfelves attacked with a maritime force on the Black fea, much too great for them to contend with. I have been told, that it is a fixed determination of the Czarina's not to conclude this war without gaining a powerful eftablifhment on the Black fea, fo that Azoph may be but one ftep to connect with further and equally important acquifitions.

If we judge from the prefent ftate of the Ruffian army, we may look for great fuccefs; for the firft foundation of it, experience, is ftrong in moft of the officers, and the men may all be called veterans. It is the fame army that faw all the campaigns againft the king of Pruf-

Pruffia, that were beat without flying at Zorndorf, and conquered at Cunnerfdorf; and that have fince been in continual action in Poland, and always victorious. It confifts of two hundred and fifty thoufand old foldiers, fixty thoufand of which are horfe, better mounted, and finer troops, than any that were ever in the Ruffian army before; with a train of artillery as fine as any in the world, and, what is of yet greater confequence, well fupplied with officers and engineers from all parts of Europe, attracted by every munificent encouragement. The Ruffians are very fenfible, that the loffes they fuftained, and their want of fuccefs is general, againft the king of Pruffia, was owing to their artillery being very badly ferved, and it has given them a great eagernefs to remedy this fatal evil; and at prefent I believe they have done it effectually; they will not any where be wanting in fuccefs on that account.

This empire has not any neighbours to whom it is not much fuperior in force, and in the conftitution of its army. Poland is at its mercy, and will continue fo till fhe is reduced to a province, an event I fhould never be much furprized at. Pruffia is not comparable in power to Ruffia, and could never make the ftand againft her arms again that we faw

in

in the laſt war; becauſe the Ruſſian army is better, more numerous, and with an artillery that yields to none in Europe; and, at the ſame time with an advantage ſhe never enjoyed before, Poland behind her, three fourths of it abſolutely in her power, to winter in, inſtead of falling back to Ruſſia, which was the caſe before. I dwell the more upon theſe particulars, becauſe it appears very clearly to me, that the next general war will ſee theſe two powers again in oppoſition, and I conjecture with very different ſucceſs.

The preſent ſtate of the Ruſſian navy promiſes alſo well to the empire; for it never ſaw ſo many hands employed in it ſince the time of Peter the Great to the preſent. New ſhips are every day launching at Petersburg, and all the old ones repairing with great expedition; a ſtout ſquadron is fitting out, of ſuch a force, that one would think the Empreſs meant to awe the Baltick, while her army is employed againſt the Turks. She has many ſhip-carpenters on the Tanais, and will be extremely formidable on the Black ſea. So that if ever Ruſſia began a war with a good proſpect of ſucceſs, it is this againſt the Turks.

There are many Engliſh at Petersburg; beſides ſeveral gentlemen in the Britiſh factory, with

with whom I became acquainted on my firſt
coming hither : there are ſo many, that I am
convinced we have more people in the Ruſſian ſervice by ſea and land, as well as in many
other departments, than is conjeċtured in England.   They certainly meet with good encouragement, or they would not be tempted to leave
their own country ; and very politick it is of
the Empreſs to avail herſelf ſo ſtrongly of the
alliance ſhe has with us ; for nothing can be
of more importance to her than getting as
many of our officers by ſea and land into her
ſervice, as poſſible ; men ſhe has in abundance, and men that will ſtand for ever to be
ſhot at ; but the deſarts of Ruſſia will not give
her experienced officers, tho' her own wars
have formed many under the tuition of foreigners.   Our engineers are of infinite conſequence to her ; and ſhe has great numbers
of ſhip-carpenters from Britain, as well as officers and common ſeamen.   There never was
a period more favourable to ſuch deſigns, than
the concluſion of the late war, in which we
had employed a greater number of forces
both by land and ſea, than we could poſſibly
keep up in peace ; ſo that very many of them
might be ſuppoſed willing enough to enter into the ſervice of a power in alliance with us ;
an

an opportunity invaluable to the Emprefs, and of which I am clear fhe made good ufe.

This caufe, with the conftant trade we carry on with Peterfburg, fills that city with Englifh, Scotch, and Irifh; but they make no great figure; which is very eafily accounted for. From what I have feen of the Ruffians, the character I had heard of them appears very juft; they are a ftrange people, that carry in all the lower claffes the marks of civility juft emerging from barbarity. They are obedient, and very patient; but have a morofenefs that feems as if it would never be tamed. The loweft among them live in conftant feverity, yet that does not feem to bow down their fpirits or activity, as flavery does in all other countries: they make nothing of hardfhips, and will bear in continuance what would deftroy in a fhort time other people of lefs robuft conftitutions. The higher claffes however fhow nothing of this. They appear in fome meafure like other people, which is the effect of luxury among them, that every where foftens and humanizes the people among whom it comes. It may be thought odd by thofe who have never been in Ruffia, that I fhould talk of luxury among the Mufcovites; but there is no court in Europe, in which (the fituation and other circumftances of the coun-

try

try confidered,) is more luxury; and particularly in the articles of drefs, equipage, fervants, and the table; which is including the
moft devouring branches of it. I have been
three times at court, which is what we commonly call very fplendid; the dreffes of every
body are more expenfive than I have any where
feen : all in gold and filver and jewels, but
fcarcely any tafte; they have in their dreffes
but one ambition, which is to be as rich as
poffible, and to have a great change; but as
to having an idea of tafte, and real elegance,
even the nobility feem not to know what it
is. They are ridiculoufly fhewy, the climate
confidered, in their coaches and fledges,
thinking, in every inftance of this fort, that
their rank can only be manifefted by an enormous expence. In their tables alfo, they are
in the fame ftile; profufe in every thing : this
has a very bad effect; for their revenues, a part
of which ought to be expended upon their
eftates in improvements, and finding employment for their neighbouring poor, are all
fquandered in the luxury of the capital, giving employment to Englifhmen, Frenchmen
and Dutchmen, inftead of their own countrymen. I know not what motive the government can have had for a long while in encouraging this profufion, unlefs it be to
keep

keep all the nobles poor, and thereby the more dependent.

The government of Ruffia is the moft abfolute in Europe; there is not even the appearance of the leaft barrier between the will of the fovereign and the people: all ranks are equally flaves to the Emprefs, not fubjects; and their punifhments fhew the fpirit of the legiflature; the greateft nobility are liable to fuffer the knout, that is, to be whipped to death; and other violent punifhments are ufed, fuch as cutting out tongues, hanging up by the ribs, and many other efforts of barbarity, which fhew the cruelty of defpotifm, without having any good effect. In the fame fpirit alfo we have feen the revolutions of the government : fcarcely a fovereign dies a natural death, but is cut off; and, by a revolution in the government, a wife, a brother, or a fifter, fixed in the throne; and all this performed by the regiments of guards, who, in fact, are pretorian cohorts, giving away the empire at their pleafure. This is ever a mark of a defpotic government, which is always infecure in proportion to its feverity.

It is amazing that politick princes, who are advanced to a throne by the favour of two or three regiments of guards, do not fee in a clearer manner, that the fame power which
gives

gives can take away ; and, the moment they
are firmly fixed in their power, do not extir-
pate the corps to whom they owe their advancement. Peter the Great faw the tendency of the Strelites and difbanded them, inftitu-
ting three regiments of guards in their place ;
but thefe guards, from not being fent to diftant
campaigns, and being conftantly around the
perfon of the fovereign, are in fact the fame
in power and opportunity as the Strelites. In
a free government, or even in an abfolute
monarchy, provided there is a fhew of fome
liberty, fuch as is in the kingdoms of France,
Spain, &c. we do not fee the guards daring to
act in this manner : but in countries of pure
defpotifm, like Ruffia, Turkey, Perfia, &c.
a prince, in order to be fafe, fhould have
no guards in particular, but all the regiments
of his army guards by turns ; and when
he is away from the capital, the garrifon of every place he is in, his guard for
the time he is there. This method, tho'
it might not infure them from all the evils
which attend defpotifm, yet it would give
them a much greater degree of fecurity than
they could poffibly be in otherwife ; which one
would apprehend an object of the firft importance.

The Roman hiftory is full of inftances of
emperors

emperors being expofed, and others fet up by
the Pretorian cohorts. Many are the Ottoman emperors who have been ftrangled by
the Janiffaries; and the hiftories of other
countries, under fimilar circumftances, abound
with the like examples ; which fhould make
thofe monarchs, that owe their advancement
to a few regiments felected from the reft of
the army, throw all their forces upon the
fame footing.

Peterfburg is tolerably gay, befides the brilliancy it derives from the court. There are a
great many concerts, in which we find numerous performers of great merit, but all Germans; here are plays alfo exhibited but irregularly, and not with agreeable circumftances ; an opera was eftablifhed, but it did
not laft long ; but by the accounts I have had,
the gala time is when parties can be made on
the ice : In winter all the country is covered
with fnow, frozen fo hard, that that is the
common feafon for travelling ; and then innumerable parties are made in fledges, which are
drawn on the frozen fnow over lakes, plains,
rivers, bogs, &c. and muft form a fpectacle
really aftonifhing to thofe who never beheld
it : I am alfo told, that this way of travelling
is fo very commodious, expeditious and agreeable, that a thoufand miles are paffed with
much

much greater eafe than an hundred at any o-
ther feafon. As I purpofe feeing the fouthern
provinces of the empire, I fhall therefore be
gone before this entertainment is to be reaped ;
but, if I can make it tolerably convenient,
will take a fhare in it on my return for Poland ; tho' I have no great idea of travelling
on fnow with any degree of information, or
even much entertainment ; for the foil, and
the cultivation of it, and the ftate of the peafants, which afford me not only inftruction
but entertainment, are then rendered invifible ;
fo that a journey full of the greateft variety
muft have then an entire famenefs. This
frozen fnow is, however, of prodigious confequence to the trade of this country ; for carriage upon it is wonderfully cheap, and more
expeditious than can well be conceived, which
is a matter of great advantage to a country
that has fuch roads as Ruffia.

The journey from Peterfburg to Pekin is
the longeft that is gone by land throughout
the world; it is near a year and half going,
and as much returning, but then it is a trading carravan, much encumbered with baggage and merchandize, and in a part of the
route with water ; for all the men and cattle
for many days are paffing fandy defarts, which
are utterly void of water. Part of this im-

Vol. III.   L   menfe

menſe route is performed on the ſnow, through a northerly part of Siberia, where there are no roads which are paſſable except on the ſnow. Of this vaſt journey, Mr. Bell in his travels has given a very good account. It is much owing to that gentleman, that the world knows any thing of Siberia, which is certainly one of the moſt extenſive countries in the world ; and, to the ſurprize of the weſtern part of Europe, conſiſts of ſeveral provinces, all of them three or four times as big as Great Britain, with a moſt fertile ſoil, and a mild climate in the ſouthern parts, capable of feeding a moſt numerous population ; but inſtead of being peopled in any proportion to its ſize, it is comparatively ſpeaking a mere deſart. But I can never be perſuaded, that it is impoſſible for a ſovereign of Ruſſia, who ſets heartily about it with judgment, activity, and penetration, to people all his dominions ; or at leaſt to put them in a way of doubling their numbers, in as ſhort a period as ever our American colonies did, for this great work, a time of profound peace would be neceſſary, and an emperor that was of a truly philoſophic diſpoſition. Liberty muſt be diffuſed, all ſlavery of the lower ranks broken through, and every man allowed to become a farmer that pleaſes.

I

I purpofed leaving Peterfburg the firft week in September, being the furtheft time I was informed that I could venture to fet out upon a long journey, unlefs I ftaid till the froft and fnow were fet in : my defign was to go to Mofcow, and from thence to Kiovia, the capital of the Ukraine, a country I was defirous of feeing. Upon making enquiries into the proper preparations for fuch a journey, I found there were but two plans ; one to travel with a carravan to Mofcow, and the other to go only with my own attendants ; of which I fhould not have lefs than five, and all well armed : That it would not be advifeable to travel with my own horfes, as I might procure a military order to be fupplied by the peafants, from poft to poft., at a fmall price ; and at the fame time the owner of the horfes would attend as a guide. In purfuance of this advice I fold my little Swedifh horfes, though fomething againft my will, and made up my guard with my own fervant, my German poftillion, and my Swede who underftood the Ruffian language, and to thefe I added by the favour of 'General Worofoff (to whom I am otherwife much indebted) two foot foldiers from his own regiment. Thefe five fellows were each of them armed with a broad fword, a pair of piftols and a carbine ; and I

L 2   carried

carried a pair of piftols and a fhort rifled bar-
rel gun, which were my arms from Denmark
through all Sweden, though I never had any
neceffity of ufing them. Thus equipped, I was
affured I might travel in perfect fafety through
all Ruffia.

CHAPTER   V.

*Journey from Peterfburg to Mofcow—Defcrip-
tion of the Country—Great Settlement of Poles
—Mofcow—Journey into The Ukraine—Account of that fine Province—Defcription of the
Agriculture of it—Culture of Hemp, Tobacco,
&c.*

I LEFT Peterfburg the 6th of September,
and with much difficulty got to Juam-
gorod, which is fifty miles, through a country
which is alternately a marfh and woods.
From thence to Novogorod took me three
days, being the diftance of one hundred
miles.   I laid both nights at Ruffian inns.   I
travelled in the character of a general officer
in the King of England's fervice, which was
of no flight ufe to me; for it is not eafy to conceive the refpect which all the lower ranks of
people pay to the military, of whatever nation,
provided they make any figure; and the number

ber of my attendants, with their being fo well armed, and the various languages we fpoke, feemed to imprefs the people with a notion that I was a perfon of very great confequence. The Ruffians have nothing in them that one can properly call civility, but I met with the moft perfect obfequioufnefs and obedience; and having provided myfelf with good bread, I lived upon excellent fifh throughout the journey. About Novogorod the country is part of it cultivated, but the inclofures are thin, and there do not feem to be any great exertions of induftry in it, but the foil appears to be a fine, deep, rich loam.

September the 11th, I got to Midna, which is above forty miles. This line of country is beautiful, being in fine but gentle inequalities, and only fprinkled with fmall woods, and well watered with rivers: there is much cultivated land; but the harveft was all got in. I faw fome crops of turneps, fuch as are common in Sweden, and as fine, but the people feem to be very miferable. Many of the peafants have farms, but then they can only work them when their landlords allow: three or four days in the week they labour on the lands of their mafters, finding fometimes cattle and implements, in confideration of being allowed the reft of their time on their

L 3 own

own farms; yet for thefe they pay a confiderable rent in products, and are befides open to the fupplying all military travellers with horfes, for which they get a very fpare allowance, and fometimes nothing at all. In a word, their ftate is fo little better than the common labourers, who work conftantly for their lords, that I did not find it a matter of envy to the latter.

The 12th I reached Thedray, a little town, prettily fituated near a river, the fame country continuing for forty-four miles, and much of it tolerably well cultivated. I paffed through feveral very extenfive plains of meadow, that appeared very fine, but were not well ftocked with cattle. The villages feem very well peopled.

The 14th I got to Twera, which is a confiderable town on the river Wolga, the diftance above eighty miles. The peafants have hitherto furnifhed me very well with horfes; yet their pay is not three farthings a mile, with fomething for the peafant. I have given to the value of four-pence Englifh for a day's journey, with which they feem to be very well fatisfied; from whence I conjecture that they ufually have nothing. This line of country is pretty well peopled. I paffed through feveral towns, and many villages, with

with some cultivated country that was cut into inclosures, and appeared to be kept in good order. Upon making enquiry, they informed me, that they cultivated barley, oats, and buck-wheat; and, from the best conjecture I can make from the intelligence they gave me, in Russian weight and measure, to the amount of between two and three quarters English per acre. All the lands that are in culture here belong to the nobility, whose agents manage them with the peasants. But some they pointed out at a distance, that belonged to others, who I found were possessors of the land, but not nobles; in other words, gentlemen. It was with some difficulty that I could get my two soldiers to behave with any decency to the peasants; they were always ready for giving them a blow, when gentle words would do to the full as well; but I curbed this licentiousness, which gave me a clear idea of the government of Russia, and at the same time convinced me, that all the Empress's fine schemes for encouraging agriculture must inevitably come to nothing. The peasant who conducted me to Twera told me, on the road, that such a track of land was his father's farm; that it belonged to him, not being hired of any landlord; and would, after his father's death, come to him.

I

I faid, then he would have an opportunity of living much better, and being more comfortable than at prefent. He replied, no; that if he got any thing, the Count Woronofkoy would take it, for there was a payment (which I took to be in the nature of a quitrent) to him out of it. I obferved feveral good tracks that were arable; he faid that his father's land was chiefly meadow, but he hired fome ploughed ground of the Count; and I found that the rent of good arable land was two fhillings an acre, that was in regular culture. But this is not a mark of great cheapnefs, the prices of all products being proportionate; for good bread is, through this country, at about a farthing a pound, and mutton and beef fomething better than three farthings, but under a penny; fo that every thing elfe muft of courfe be proportionate. And a farmer muft cultivate a large track of ground to raife a fmall fum of money; but the cafe is, that money is fo valuable, that they raife no more products than neceffary for their common purchafes and rent, and the fmall fum they bring anfwers where all things are proportioned. I found from this man's account, that a farmer, who lived upon his own eftate, was at the mercy of the neareft nobleman, and, if he grew rich, would furely
be

be fleeced by him. It is impossible to introduce improvements into such a country without an entire new system.

As I advanced in my journey, I every where
made enquiries after new settlements on the
lands belonging to the Empress; but heard
nothing of them till I got to Twera: there
they told me, that in the forest of Volkoufkile,
about an hundred miles to the south-west,
was a very large new colony of Poles, settled
at the expence of the Czarina. I immediately determined to go out of my way to view
it, that I might have an opportunity to see in
what manner they were fixed, and what a
reception they met with. I got there the
16th, passing through a country, the chief of
which is waste, being either forest or meadow, but with few villages. I found the
settlement of Poles consisted of about six hundred families; and pleased me better than
any thing I had seen in Russia. Each family
has a small, but not a bad house, built of
wood, and covered with shingles; a house as
good or better than the generality of small
farm-houses in England, where the mud
walls would give foreigners an idea that we
were the poorest nation in Europe. Behind
every house was an inclosure of about fifty
English acres in one field. The fence was a
ditch

ditch and parapet, with a row of young plants for a hedge, that feemed to be a kind of elm. Each inclofure came down to a rivulet, where cattle might water. Each family had two fheep, and a ram, to a certain number, a cow, and a couple of oxen to till the arable, with a cart and a plough; all which were at the Emprefs's expence, and do not coft what they would in England. This may be conceived, when I give the rates. Two oxen for ploughing and carting come to but five pounds; a cow to thirty fhillings; a fheep eighteen-pence; a plough four fhillings; a cart nine fhillings; each houfe coft the Emprefs about four and twenty fhillings; and every family had an allowance of provifion the firft year from the neighbouring country, which coft her nothing; fo that the total expence, per family, was only eight pounds ten fhillings; and many of the families confift of eight or nine perfons. The farms were all under culture, and fubdivided by the people themfelves; and I obferved that thefe inner fences were done exactly in the fame manner as the furrounding ones. Some had four fields, others five, and fome fix. The land, when they fettled it, was wafte foreft, but not many trees on it, that yielded a wild and luxuriant grafs: it is a red loam on clay. The peafants

4

peafants cultivate wheat without exception, which they had been ufed to in Poland ; each had one field of it ; alfo a crop of barley, oats, or rice ; with a piece of beans, and another of turneps. Their farms were in general in good order, and they feemed to be extremely diligent and induftrious in their management. Some of them had vaftly in-creafed their cattle, keeping as many as they pleafed on the adjoining foreft : fome had more than twenty fheep, ten cows, and fix oxen ; but they had greatly increafed their farms, which .the Emprefs allows, provided the former portion is all in culture. They all feemed to be perfectly happy, being en-tirely free from all oppreffion by being on the lands of the crown ; and there is no doubt but they will in time yield a fine revenue, without any feverity being employed.

Some of them had pieces of hemp, which thrives with them fo well, that its culture increafes among them daily. I enquired particularly into the value of an acre, and found that it was worth upon the fpot from fifty fhillings to four pounds, which I think is very confiderable, and fhews that thefe new colonies may prove a fource of very great wealth and population.

It

It is extremely evident from this inftance, that the way of bringing improvements to bear in Ruffia, is not by encouragements given to the peafants, unlefs they could at once be fet as free as in other countries, which I am convinced already is an impoffibility, from what I have feen on this journey; becaufe the nobility and other land-owners, to whom they are vaffals, fleece and opprefs them to fuch a degree, that they can never be fecure of any property, unlefs their encouragement comes from their own lords. Even they who are not vaffals, but have poffeffions of their own, are trampled on by the foldiery. No improvement, by giving them a greater degree of liberty, can therefore have any effect, unlefs it comes from their lords; as in this cafe of the Polifh emigrants. The Emprefs fixing them upon the crown-lands, they are vaffals of the crown, and all the liberty fhe chufes to give them they will fecurely enjoy, without any one's daring to injure them in any refpect; and as the fovereign can never profitably cultivate an extenfive domain for her own account, this is the only means of working improvements; and they cannot fail of proving moft highly profitable.

And the nobility have it alfo in their power to make the fame improvements upon their

own

own eftates, becaufe under their protection the peafants would be fecure. But as to all general improvements in hufbandry, it is merely impoffible that they fhould be attended with the leaft effect. Every landlord has every thing in his power upon his own lands, provided, I mean, he be of rank and confequence; and they have the ability, by means of the flavery of their peafants, to work very great effects, if they pleafed to undertake them. Laws or edicts therefore muft be directed to them ; the rewards for a proper conduct fhould all be granted to them ; the Emprefs fhould addrefs herfelf to them, and let them find favour at court in proportion to the cultivation of their eftates : thefe are the only means of doing great things.

The crown lands are fo amazingly extenfive, that very great things might in this manner be done, and far more effectually than by general laws, in a country where the people are fo habituated to flavery, that it would be a vain attempt to free them under all mafters. Thefe fix hundred families had at once thirty thoufand acres in culture, befides the increafe, which by many of them was very confiderable; all which will, in procefs of time, yield a great revenue to the crown, befides the acquifition of ftrength which

which the empire receives by the addition of population, and the amount of fo much induftry as all thefe people create. After five years this colony is to pay an annual rent, which in ten more will be increafed, and after that remain a freehold to the Poles, fubject only to that rent. An idea of the field which the Emprefs has for improvement may be conjectured by one contiguous track of wafte and foreft, partly in the Ziranni province, which contains above thirty-feven millions of Englifh acres, and belongs to the crown, befides tracks in Siberia and Tartary ten times as large. It is therefore extremely evident, that the great object of Ruffian politicks fhould be the peopling and cultivating the crown lands; which, if managed with unremitted diligence, and without fparing expence, might be continually on the improvement, and in fuch fwift manner, that the quantity of land rendered profitable might foon be immenfely great.

This colony of Poles have a market in the middle of their fettlement on the great road, where merchants refort to buy their fpare products, hemp, &c. bringing all thofe forts of commodities which they want; and this trade occafions a circulation among them which is highly advantageous. The report of of the indulgence and benefits they have met with has had great effect in Poland; so that they pointed out to me a track of land contiguous, where they soon expected two hundred families more. Having viewed several farms of the settlers and made such enquiries as I thought necessary, I set out for Moscow without returning to Twera: the distance is one hundred and seventeen miles; and I arrived there the 20th, passing through a very finely variegated country, well watered and wooded, and spread in fine plains, with many villages scattered through them; and much appearance of cultivation: all this country is in the hands of three or four nobles, whose stewards direct the management of it.

This city is the greatest in the empire; it was once strongly fortified for this part of the world, but the security of the present times has made every thing unnecessary except a wall: It is about sixteen miles in circumference, and contains about half a million of inhabitants, till lately the Czars spent a part of the year here; but the palace, which is a very indifferent one, having been damaged by fire, they have not of late years been there; but notwithstanding this, Moscow is the residence of a vast number of the nobility, indeed of three fourths of those whose offices

or

or expectations do not oblige them to attend the court ; in which inftance there is a greater appearance of liberty than in moft other countries ; for in general, all the nobility of a kingdom flock to the feat of government.

Mofcow is very irregularly built ; but it is a beautiful city, from the windings of the river, and from many eminences which are covered with groves of fine tall trees, and from numerous gardens, and lawns, which opening to the water give it a moft pleafing airy appearance. I expected to fee nothing but wooden houfes, but was agreeably furprized at the fight of many very fine fabricks of brick and ftone. It is beyond comparifon a finer city than Peterfburg. The number of churches and chapels, amounting it is faid to eighteen hundred, make a great figure in the printed defcriptions of this city; but from the appearance of them I fhould fuppofe the fact falfe, and that out of great numbers very few are worthy of note. I faw the great bell, which is the largeft in the world, and indeed a moft ftupendous thing it is. They have many other bells in the city, which much exceed any thing that is elfewhere to be met with ; the Ruffians being remarkably fond of this ornament of their churches.

There

There is a very confiderable manufacture at Mofcow of various hemp fabricks; particularly, fail cloth and fheeting, which employs fome thoufands of looms, and many thoufands of people; the hemp is moft of it brought from the Ukraine: there are alfo great numbers of confiderable merchants here, who carry on a very extenfive commerce with all parts of the empire; for there is water carriage from hence to the Black and Cafpian feas, and with but few interruptions to the Baltick alfo, which are circumftances that make it the center of a very great commerce.

This city is much better fituated for the metropolis of the empire than Peterfburg: It is almoft in the center of the moft cultivated parts of it; communicating in the manner above-mentioned with the three inland feas, not at a great diftance from the moft important province of the empire, the Ukraine; open to the fouthern territories on the Black fea, and by means of the rivers Wolga and the Don commanding an inland navigation of prodigious extent. Its vicinity alfo to the countries, which muft always be the feat of any wars with the Turks, the enemies moft to be attended to of all thofe with whom the Ruffians wage war; upon the whole made it infinitely a better fituation for the feat of government, than that of Peterſburg, which is at the very extremity of the empire, and poſſeſſing few of theſe advantages. Founding that city, and making it the ſeat of foreign commerce and naval power, was an admirable exertion of genius; but the ſeat of government ſhould always have been at Moſcow.

The 23d I left that city, taking the road towards Ukraine—I was fortunate in having very fine clear weather, and found the roads every where exceedingly good, no autumnal rains having yet fallen. I got that night to Molaſky, the diſtance about ſixty miles, nor did I find ſuch a day's journey too much for the horſes; the country all this way is a level plain, very fertile, and much of it well cultivated, with many villages, and in general, a well peopled territory: the peaſants ſeemed tolerably eaſy, but ſcarcely any of them have any property! From Molaſky, fifty ſix miles carried me the next day to Arcroiſy, a ſmall town; ſituated in a territory not ſo well-peopled as the preceding; the villages thinner, and but little of the ſoil cultivated, being covered with much timber of great ſize and beauty. The 25th I reached Demetriovitz, at the diſtance of more than fifty miles, every ſtep of which was acroſs a foreſt in which I ſaw not the leaſt veſtige of any habitation: the road was not difficult to find, even

if

if I had not had a guide, but it is not much frequented ; the mercantile people making this part of the journey to the Ukraine by wa-ter : This immenfe track of wild country, is part open meadow and part covered with tim-ber, which would in England be thought a glorious fight : the foil is all a fine fand, and, if I may judge from the fpontaneous vegetation, a moft fertile loam ; fo that nothing is want-ing but an induftrious population : but with-out that, the whole territory is of little worth. I baited the horfes in the middle of the foreft, and refrefhed myfelf and company, much admiring the uncommon extent of coun-try that was without the leaft appearance of being inhabited : I apprehended that the coun-try muft have a great refemblance of the boundlefs plains and woods of Louifiana.

The 26th I rode forty miles through an uninhabited plain to Serenfky ; no timber in it, but all one level fertile meadow. I faw fome herds of cattle feeding as if wild, but the land was not a tenth part ftocked; for the grafs, if we turned out of the road, was up al-moft to the bellies of the horfes ; fuch mea-dow would, I apprehend, in any part of En-gland let readily for five and twenty fhillings an acre, yet here of no value : fuch are the effects of population, liberty, and induftry !

M 2   The

The fame diftance the 27th. carried me to Brenſky, a pretty little town on the banks of a river in the middle of a foreſt ; a place truly romantick. I felt myſelf rather fatigued with hard riding ſince I left Peterſburg, and therefore reſted myſelf here the 28th, left a continuance of this great exerciſe ſhould give me a fit of illneſs, for which Ruſſia is the moſt unfit place in the world ; for every man out of Peterſburg and Moſcow muſt be his own phyſician.

The 29th I got to Staradoff at the diſtance of fifty miles : full twenty of which are through a rich and pleaſant country, much of it very well cultivated ; they were getting in part of their harveſt : they cultivate all the grain and pulſe common in England; and from what I ſaw I have little doubt but their huſbandry is extremely good. They generally manage their lands in the ſyſtem of ſowing firſt hemp, then oats, then turneps, then wheat or rye, but much of the former is ſown : after this huſbandry of five years which is ſometimes varied to ſix or ſeven two crops of hemp being taken they leave the land fallow for three four or five years ; by fallow is not however meant ploughing it all that time, but letting it run to graſs and weeds : it is preſently covered thickly ; the ſecond year all the weeds

2   diſappear,

difappear, and they have a very fine meadow, without the trouble of fowing any hay feeds, which they keep as the feeding ground of their farms for feveral years, as their cattle require ; and whenever they plough it up again.they are fure to find a field entirely fertilized and ready to yield abundant crops. I fhould have apprehended that this management would have filled the land with the feeds of weeds, which, upon breaking it up, would have deftroyed their crop ; but an agent that feemed to belong to fome man of a large eftate anfwered me by faying that the firft crop they fowed, being hemp, entirely cleaned the ground for all the fucceffive ones ; that in cafe the effect was not perfected, a fecond would infallibly do it ; for I found they had an idea here, that hemp is a great cleaner of the land, and that no weeds can live among it ; which is what I do not re-collect any writer of hufbandry mentions, as being the practice of Englifh farmers. It is one inftance, among many others I have met with, in which I regret not making myfelf better acquainted with the hufbandry of England, before I made en-quiries into that of other countries. The quantity of hemp fown in all this country is very confiderable ; indeed I was told, that this province, which joins a part of the Ukraine in

M 3   fome

some places, is much like that country, only the
soil not quite so fine. The land here is a rich
loam, wet, and much inclinable to a clay. They
reckon an acre of hemp, one year with another, to be worth three pounds ; an acre of
wheat yields three quarters, and as much of
rye ; four quarters of barley, and as much or
more of oats.   They have fine crops of beans
about five quarters upon an acre.   They do
not cultivate so many turneps as they should,
but trust many of their cattle all winter long
on the waste, where they find herbage enough,
notwithstanding the snow, to keep them alive :
but it would certainly be much better husbandry to keep them better, and collect their dung.
They have large herds, which in summer are
kept in fine order by means of the exceeding
good pasturage, which all the meadows yield in
vast plenty. All this country belongs to different
noblemen, and is cultivated by their stewards and agents, who seem to know their
business very well ; but the peasants seem to
be very poor, having scarcely any signs
of cultivation around their cottages, and yet
they are fed by what they raise for themselves
on certain days.   I remark, that the peasants
in this empire are in general happy in proportion to the neglect under which the country lies ; in the midst of vast wastes and fo-

rests

refts they feem to be tolerably eafy; but any tracks well cultivated, are done at their expence, and they appear very near on the fame rank, as the blacks in our fugar colonies.

From Staradoff to Czernicheu is feventy five miles, which I rode in two days, arriving there the 1ft of November. Part of this track is as well cultivated as that on the other fide of Staradoff, but much of it is covered with foreft. I obferved hemp in many of the fields, and fome of it was not yet pulled, though the harveft was generally in. Czernicheu is a very well built town, finely fituated on the banks of the river Defna, which is navigable for barges of fifty tons, is very well fortified, and inhabited by about fifteen thoufand people; many of whom carry on a confiderable trade with Kiovia, and, by the Nieper, with Poland. All the track of country, which lies upon the river Defna, is very rich, and well cultivated. Many of the inhabitants of Czernicheu are Coffack Tartars; but a traveller has no more reafon to fear them, than the inhabitants of any other part of Ruffia; for the government, although milder in the Ukraine, and the neighbouring provinces, from having been conquered from Poland, is yet the fame, and the police as ftrict

M 4 as

as in any other part of the empire. I made enquiries here concerning the danger of travelling through the Ukraine in this time of war; and they assured me, that whether it was war or peace, I should not see the least appearance of any danger; that I should find the Ukraine, tho' inhabited by Tartars, as well a regulated province as any county in England. They said, there had been no incursions made into any of these provinces, as the theatre of the war was pushed on to the countries around the Black sea, and where they doubted not but it would continue.

November the 3d I reached Kiovia, the capital of the Ukraine, and fourscore miles from Czernicheu. The road leads on the banks of the Desna, through a beautiful country; great part of it being well-peopled and cultivated. It is inhabited by Tartarian descendants; but I found the present Cossacks, who have very little idea of husbandry, come far from the eastward, from countries that reach to the river Don, at the distance of above a thousand miles from hence. The present race of the Ukraine are a civilized people, and the best husbandmen in the Russian empire.

Kiovia, one of the most considerable cities I have seen in Russia, is a place well known in

the

the hiftory of that empire; for tho' it has been fubject to many revolutions, which reduced it to a low ftate compared with its former grandeur, yet it has now recovered all thofe antient blows; it is well built of brick and ftone: the ftreets are wide and ftrait, and well paved; it has a very noble cathedral, much of it lately rebuilt, and eleven other churches. It has forty thoufand inhabitants; and is ftrongly fortified. The Nieper is here a noble river; and feveral larger rivers falling into it, after wafhing fome of the richeft provinces of Poland, enable this town to carry on a very confiderable commerce. It is the grand magazine of all the commodities of the Ukraine, particularly hemp and flax, which in this fine province are raifed in greater quantities, and of a better quality, than in any other part of Europe. The Ukraine is the richeft province in the Ruffian empire. Part of it formerly was a province of Poland, and the reft an independent fovereignty, under a Tartar prince; but the whole is now a mere province of Ruffia, and much the richeft acquifition that crown has made. It is upon an average two hundred and fifty miles long eaft to weft; and one hundred and forty broad north to fouth.

November

November 5th, I left the capital of this province; and as I purposed making a circular detour of the western part, I went to Buda that day, which is about fifty miles ; most of the country rich and very well cultivated ; the soil is a black loam, and they raise in it the various sorts of grain and pulse that are commonly met with in England. I passed through great tracks of stubble ground, from off which the wheat, barley, and oats were carried. And I observed numerous hemp grounds, though not so much of the country is under that crop as corn ; in some villages where I made enquiries, they spoke nothing but the Polish language, and of a dialect which my interpreter for the Russian knew nothing of, though he had assured me he understood Polish very well ; but I met with other peasants who spoke Russian, and they informed me that their products of hemp arose in value sometimes to six pounds an acre, but three or four pounds were a common crop ; of wheat four quarters; barley five, and oats and beans six, and sometimes more an acre ; which appeared to me to be all very considerable quantities. Their grounds are most of them inclosed with ditches, to some of which are hedges, but not to all. They have fine meadow grounds, which they convert to hemp, in the manner I related above,

bove, but leave them under grafs for ten or twelve years before they break them up; and keep them in a tillage-management as long: upon fome grounds they have three crops of hemp running. Flax they alfo cultivate, but they do not reckon it fo profitable as hemp. In the management of their cattle they are very good farmers: they have large ftocks, and they houfe them all whenever the fnow is above four inches deep upon the ground; they litter them down well with ftraw, and feed them with hay or turneps: cows are their principal ftock; and they fell immenfe quantities of butter and cheefe, though it is extremely remarkable, that not many years ago they knew not what butter was. The property of all this country is very much divided; here are very few great eftates belonging to nobility: the old inhabitants of the country were very free, and had a great equality among them; and this in poffeffions as well as other circumftances; and fortunately this continues, though in fubjection to Ruffia, moft of the peafants are little farmers, whofe farms are their own, with ten times the liberty among them that I any where elfe faw in Ruffia; the government are extremely cautious of oppreffing or offending them, for they never will be in want of

folicitations

folicitations from the Turks to join the Tartars in alliance with the Porte. They pay a
confiderable tribute, but raife it among themfelves according to their own cuftoms; and
they alfo furnifh the Ruffian armies with a
great many very faithful troops. Thefe points,
with the immenfe value of the trade the Ruffians carry on by means of their products,
hemp and flax in particular, render the province of the firft importance. I paffed in this
line of fifty miles, great numbers of villages
and fcattered farms.

Buda is a little town, or rather a large village, prettily fituated between two rivers in a
country perfectly pleafant. I turned off to
the north-weft and got the 6th to Kordyne,
a little town fifty two miles from Buda: All
this country is equal to the preceding day's
journey; I never faw a track of land that
had more refemblance to the beft parts of England. Nothing could be more fortunate than
the weather for my expedition; the rains u-
fually come very heavy the middle of September, and foon after them frofts and fnow, but
I have yet had a conftant azure fky, with
warm winds. If it holds five days more, I
fhall have paffed this province, and I do not
hear that there is any thing worthy of notice
between the Ukraine and Peterfburg, therefore

fore the weather will not be fo effential to the journey. I remarked in the country I paffed to day, feveral tobacco plantations; they re-femble hop grounds when the hillocks are not poled; they reckon it as profitable as hemp, which is owing I believe to the ready vent they find for all they cultivate; the Tartars upon the Black fea, and the Kalmucks buy large quantities; and they are not fo nice in the feparation of the forts, as our planters in Virginia are obliged to be, though they fell their product for as good a price; but I do not think there grows the lefs hemp on account of their tobacco; it feems to be cultivated, in-ftead of fowing quite fo much corn as in other parts; an acre of tobacco is worth five pounds in a good year. They have large houfes highly run up for drying it. They think the land cannot be too rich for either hemp or to-bacco, and accordingly plant them on frefh land.

The 7th I reached Lefzozyn, at the di-ftance of fix and thirty miles, the country continuing the fame; much hemp and to-bacco being planted through the whole: At a village by the way where I ftopped to make enquiries, I found they preferred a red clay for their hemp, and planted all the black mold with tobacco. I obferved many ploughs

at

at work, fome with fix horfes, of a little weak breed, but in general each was drawn by four ftout oxen. They were turning up wheat ftubbles, and faid they ploughed them before winter, that the frofts and fnow might improve the ground, which feems to be good management. I think I never faw fuch deep ploughing as thefe peafants give their ground: I meafured nine inches perpendicular after a plough drawn by four oxen; what the depth is in England I never noticed particularly, but believe it is not fo much as this. Their ploughs are very well conftructed; if I may judge by their entirely turning over the land, they are all of iron, having no wood about them; a fort I had never feen till I came into the Ukraine; nor have they any wheels which our plough-wrights in England think fo effential. I remarked here feveral very noble crops of cabbages, and in fuch vaft quantities, that I concluded they muft feed their cattle with them, and was right in the conjecture : they ufed formerly to cultivate only the Swedifh turnep for this purpofe, but cabbages (they are a red fort, and come to a monftrous fize, 25 or 30 lb. for inftance) by degrees have come into fafhion among them, fo as to be the crop on which they entirely depend, with help of hay for the winter fuftenance of their cattle. They
fow

fow the feed early in the fpring, and plant them
when of a proper fize, into the field in rows,
and afterwards keep them as clean as they do
their tobacco, by conftant hoeing: an acre
of them will winter four or five large oxen;
they reckon the culture extremely profitable.
They have alfo whole fields of potatoes, fome
for their own ufe, and fome for fale, there
being a great demand for them at Ockzacow,
on the Black fea, whither they are fent by
water; but I cannot help thinking they muft
have a fort unknown in England: I rode into
a field where a crop was taking up, and great
numbers were as large as the body of a quart
bottle; I never faw fuch before. They freely
gave me a few of thefe large ones to take
away for feed; they are planted by flices in
the fame manner as ours: the peafants here
think that lands of moderate fertility do for
them. Such a potatoe, I fhould apprehend,
might, for feeding cattle, be made of very
great advantage to the hufbandry of England;
they yield from twelve to fifteen hundred
bufhels per acre.

The 8th I rode to Kwafowa, a large
village, the diftance about forty miles.
This country is, in fome places, a continued level plain; in others it is variegated
with gentle hills, which never rife into

moun-

mountains, but are cultivated to the tops. Hemp and tobacco are common crops through the whole, and alfo fome flax, but not in equal quantities. All the country is divided into fmall eftates, or rather farms, cultivated by the owners; though I am told that in fome parts of the province to the fouth, where I have not been, there are large eftates belonging to the nobles, and that thofe parts are not near fo well peopled or cultivated as thefe parts; which is a ftrong proof that much of the good hufbandry met with in the Ukraine is owing to the peafants being owners of their lands, and vaffalage almoft unknown in the province. It cannot be doubted but the Emprefs may bring the crown lands of Ruffia, on all the frontier of Poland, into as flourifhing a ftate as parts of this province, if fhe encourages foreign fettlers with all the fpirit fhe has hitherto fhewn, fince it is in her power to give them all the advantages which the inhabitants of the Ukraine enjoy. They have, it is true, a noble country, equal, I think, in foil, &c. to Flanders, and almoft as well cultivated; but I have feen in other provinces of this empire immenfe wafte tracks of land, not at all inferior in every thing derived from nature; but enflaved peafants are utterly inconfiftent with a flourifhing hufbandry.

The

The 9th I got to Norodiza, the diſtance forty miles : the ſoil in this track is inferior to what I have paſſed; but the people appear to be excellent huſbandmen : they have ſome hemp, but little tobacco, only a plantation here and there. I paſſed through ſeveral villages, which have been lately built by fugitive Poles, who have fixed themſelves here on ſome ſmall waſtes, by leave of the government, but without any expence. The 10th I had a very hard day's journey to Belechoka, the diſtance more than ſixty miles, and the road in ſome places marſhy. Only parts of this track are well cultivated, but no hemp, flax, or tobacco are raiſed ; there are alſo ſome waſtes, but they will not be ſuch long, for the Poles are planting themſelves on them very faſt. Here I paſſed out of the province of Ukraine.

It is this territory which raiſes nineteenths of the hemp and flax which we import at ſuch a vaſt expence from Ruſſia; it is therefore deſerving of a little attention; for the beſt politicians, who have given moſt attention to the affairs of our American colonies, have all of them inſiſted very ſtrenuouſly upon the poſſibility and even eaſe of ſupplying ourſelves totally from thence. What truth there is in this I know not; but it will be of uſe to conſider this province of the Ukraine with more attention than any writer has hitherto done, becaufe from knowing it perfectly we may judge how far we can reafon by analogy when America is fpoken of; and this is the more neceffary, as the accounts which have hitherto been publifhed of it are ftrangely contradictory; for on one hand they tell us truly, that the Ruffian hemp comes from thence; but on the other, they give fuch a picture of the ftate of the country, that one would fuppofe it poffeffed by herds of wandering Coffacks, which is utterly inconfiftent with the idea of fuch a ftate of agriculture as is neceffary for making fo great a proficiency in the culture of hemp and flax. All thefe accounts muft have been copied one from another, and the firft of them at leaft a century and half old. To be convinced of which, let any perfon look into the account of the Ukraine, in that very judicious collection of voyages and travels, entitled *Harris's*; there he will meet with mention indeed of the great fertility of the country, but three-fourths of the particulars given are relative to its wandering Tartar inhabitants; and the words hemp or flax never once ufed; and a defcription of the people given that would be utterly inconfiftent with fuch agriculture; and this is the cafe with all the books that I have

turned

turned to; but the reason muſt be, the
country's being ſo extremely out of the way of
all travellers, that not a perſon in a century
goes to it, who takes notes of his obſervations
with intention to lay them before the world :
very few ſuch go even to Peterſburg; now
and then one croſſes Ruſſia towards Perſia;
but all keep a thouſand or two of miles from
the Ukraine; and hence it is that the greateſt
changes happen in ſuch remote parts of the
world, without any thing of the matter being
known. And our writers of geography, who
are every day publiſhing, copy each other
in ſo ſlaviſh a manner, that a fact in 1578 is
handed down to us as the only information
we can have in 1769; a circumſtance which
reigns in all the books of general geography
that I have ſeen. Let me here add, that I
have, in travelling to gain information, viſited
thoſe countries about which it would be in
vain to conſult books; for, Holland and
Flanders alone excepted, all the reſt of the preſent journey is through countries, the former
accounts of which are entirely falſe, not from
errors in the authors, but from great changes
that have happened in a long courſe of years.
But to return.

It has been ſuppoſed that hemp and flax,
coming to us from ſo northern a place as Pe-

terſburg, would grow in the midſt of perpetual
froſts and ſnows; but though we import it
from latitude 60, yet it all grows in the
Ukraine, which lies between latitude 47 and
52, and is beſides as fine, mild a climate as
any in Europe: this is the latitude of the ſouth
of France; and with theſe advantages, the ſoil
is ſuperior to moſt I have ſeen, being in general a very rich, deep mould, between a loam
and a dry clay, but without any of that tenacious ſtickineſs which is ſo diſagreeable in
moving through a clay country in England.
I am clear in the importance of conveying a
preciſe idea, when we ſpeak of ſoils; but
not having been uſed to practical huſbandry
ſo much as I wiſh I had, I cannot properly
make uſe of the neceſſary technical terms.
To theſe advantages, which this province enjoys, I ſhould certainly add, whether from
accident or natural ingenuity, their good huſbandry, which is much ſuperior to any thing
that I have ſeen ſince I left Flanders.

After giving theſe particulars, we may ex-
amine, upon a good foundation, the capability
of our colonies affording hemp and flax in
equal quantities. Thoſe gentlemen who have
travelled through them, beſt know how well
they anſwer to the above deſcription: but if I
may be permitted to ſpeak on the authorities
which

which many modern relations give us,
the settlements on the sea-coasts of North-
America will never yield hemp in any quantities; the climate is much too changeable
and severe; sharp cutting frosts are met with
in Carolina, in 30 degrees of latitude, and a
burning sun, equal in heat to any part of the
world: in New-England, Nova-Scotia, &c.
where hemp has been attempted, it has always failed, from the severity of the climate,
and the badness of the lands. But all accounts
give a very contrary description of the countries on the Missisippi: from the descriptions
which I have read of the track on that river,
from lat. 33 to lat. 40, I should apprehend it
to be, of all other places in America, the most
adapted to this culture: for the soil is rich,
black, and very deep; the climate much more
regular and pleasant than on the sea-coast,
which is all marshes and swamps, and the
lands in immense plenty, and all fresh.
Hemp certainly might be raised in those parts
to great advantage, provided the descriptions
of them, which we have had, are just; which
I do not see any reason to doubt. But then
the misfortune is, that these beautiful tracks
of country are without inhabitants; and great
numbers of people are necessary for an advantageous culture of hemp. Another circum-

N 3 stance

ſtance to be conſidered is, the profit of ſuch
an application of the land : hemp would never
be cultivated to any purpoſe in Carolina, or
our ſouthern colonies, if the climate was proper, becauſe rice and indico, and I believe
even cotton, pay the planter much ſuperior
profits ; and if indico and cotton were introduced on the Miſſiſſippi, as in all probability
they would be, hemp would be neglected till
thoſe markets failed which took off the more
beneficial articles. But, on the other hand,
we ought not to regret this, for the national
profit is proportionably greater : the more
the planter's advantage, the more the national
income is increaſed. Hemp in fact is not
an article of culture that is comparable to
many others in profit, and will conſequently
never be cultivated except in thoſe countries
where corn and pulſe, and other leſs profitable articles, would occupy the land if that
did not ; but when the ſoil and climate will
do for richer commodities, it is idle to ſup-
poſe that poorer ones will be attended to.

If, therefore, it is an eſſential point to raiſe
all the hemp in our colonies which we bring
from Ruſſia, new plantations muſt be formed
on the Miſſiſſippi, in a latitude that will not
do for the rich American ſtaples ; ſuch for
inſtance as that of 37 to 40, or thereabouts.
The

The country so included is one of the finest in the world for all common husbandry; so that the inhabitants, like those of the Ukraine, would very easily raise all the necessaries of life, at the same time that their principal attention was given to hemp as their staple.

C H A P T E R   VI.

Journey to Petersburg through the Frontiers of Poland—Observations on the State of several Provinces — Russian Acquisitions —Remarks on the War between the Russians and the Turks—Journey to Archangel, and through Lapland—Return to Petersburg—Livonia.

NOVEMBER the 11th I left Belachoka, and rode to Rzeezyka, at the distance of forty-four miles, through a country very different from the Ukraine; for it consists of little besides marshes, with but few inhabitants. It is to be noted, that most of this track is in Poland, and Rzeezyka is the capital of a province once Polish, and which all the maps I have lay down as a part of Poland; but I am convinced there have been strange changes wrought by force of Russian arms on the frontiers of that kingdom. The town is large, populous, and

N 4   strongly

ftrongly fortified; but as much Ruffian as
Mofcow.   Here are great numbers of Poles,
it is true; but all the houfes which the war
had emptied are filled up carefully with Ruffian families; and there is a Ruffian garrifon,
Ruffian government, and, in a word, fcarcely
any thing Polifh in it.   By this extreme political conduct, that empire makes very great
acquifitions on the fide of Poland, without
the world knowing any thing of the matter;
which is the effect of the miferable government, or rather anarchy, under which they
live; and which is the pretence for the Ruffian troops fwarming over the whole kingdom; fo that three parts in four of it are
a province of Ruffia, and probably the
whole will in a little time, which may
be more advantageous to the kingdom;
for no defpotifm of the Eaft is fo great a curfe
to a people, as the furious military anarchy
that reigns at prefent in Poland.   I have received accounts from various people fince I
have been in Ruffia, from which I fhould
apprehend, that full half the inhabitants of
that great country have been cut off and
ftarved within thefe ten years.   Near half the
kingdom is abfolutely in the hands of the
Ruffians, who receive pretty heavy taxes from
it, and alfo recruits for their army againft
the

the Turks: vaſt numbers of people are, by this means, alſo tranſported into Ruſſia; for Poliſh noblemen, who declare againſt the Ruſſian party, are driven entirely from their eſtates, and great numbers of their peaſants removed immediately into Ruſſia, with their cattle and all their effects; ſo that the Empreſs may eaſily have increaſed her ſubjects in the degree which I was told, at Peterſburg. And it certainly muſt be allowed, that the cards ſhe plays in this manner enſure her a game uncommonly advantageous. The poor Poles, driven about, and reduced to the utmoſt miſery by their own people, muſt be very ready to fix upon lands in Ruſſia, and be vaſſals only to the Empreſs. If this ſcene of confuſion therefore laſts much longer in Poland, that kingdom will be entirely depopulated, and the Ruſſian provinces filled with people; an event ſilently taking place, and which will increaſe this formidable power more than half a dozen victories over the Turks.

From Rzeezyka I followed the courſe of the Nieper to Rohakzow, where I arrived the 12th; the diſtance more than fifty miles. The country is an open level plain, of fine meadow. I ſaw numerous villages deſerted; and the fields, formerly arable, become paſture,

ture, but without cattle to graze them: all the inhabitants were moved into Ruffia. That town is the capital of a large province, the whole of which is in the hands of the Ruffians, who have three ftrong fortreffes in it, well garrifoned. Rohakzow is a fine town, beautifully fituated on the Nieper, on which its prefent mafters carry on a confidera- ble commerce. I much fufpect, from the fortifications raifed here by the Ruffians, whe- ther the town or province will ever more be in the hands of the Poles. I was informed here, that much the greateft part of the province of Minfki, one of the moft confiderable in Li- thuania, is entirely quiet, and in the abfolute power of the Ruffians ; and where it will end, time can only know ; but the prefent ftate of affairs in all this part of the world looks on every fide only in favour of the Ruffians ; and it is certainly a moft ftrange infatuation, that the other powers of Europe fhould be mere ftanders-by, and look on to this great fuccefs of the Ruffians without thinking it their in- tereft to interfere. Auftria and Pruffia are armed, it is true ; but the progrefs of this empire is of a kind which admits not open declarations from any but the Poles. I have heard it mentioned as a mark of very faga- cious politicks in the Turks, that the real
reafon

reafon of the prefent war with Ruffia is from a jealoufy of the Mufcovite power being too much increafed by the advantages taken of the troubles in Poland. The Porte thought there was danger of the Emprefs taking pof-feffion of the whole kingdom of Poland in her own name; and judged that the beft way of preventing fuch a great acceffion to her power was by the fword cutting her out work elfe-where.

From Rohakzow, I reached Rychow the 13th; the diftance more than forty miles. All this country is very rich, and part of it very well cultivated, but it is in the hands of the Ruffians entirely; many of the peafants are of that nation, and every thing feen is a proof that this empire has much enlarged its bounds, without either a formal war, or even the authority of a treaty. This place is in the province of Miflau, a very fine and fertile country, an hundred miles long, and as many broad, and all in the hands of the Ruffians. The foil here is chiefly a reddifh loam; much of it is in culture, as was evident from the large tracks of ftubble I went through; but I faw no hemp, flax, or tobacco, thofe produdts being pretty much confined to the Ukraine. Rychow, with fome neighbouring towns, be-long to a Polifh nobleman, driven away by
the

the Ruffians, who have feized his whole eftate, and taken poffeffion of it in a manner that precludes the idea of his ever returning. From this place I rode about forty miles to Kudzin, through the fame province. All this line of country, I could fee, had been in general under culture, but it was now entirely wafte. I counted the remains of no lefs than feven villages, which were entirely deferted, all the inhabitants being fled to Ruffia. From Kudzin, the fame diftance brought me, on the 15th, to Krula, another little town, with a Ruffian garrifon. The country is partly cultivated, and partly deferted; but the remaining inhabitants will not be left here long; for I faw a Ruffian commandant, whofe bufinefs was, the taking an account of the people of feveral adjacent villages that had petitioned for lands in Ruffia. Thefe emigrations are not at all furprizing: in time of peace the Polifh nobles treat all the peafants as flaves in the utmoft extent of the word: when, therefore, a fcene of trouble and confufion comes, they are fure to take the firft opportunity to defert, that they may efcape in future the renewal of their former mifery; and the condition of the new fettlers in Ruffia is fo infinitely fuperior to that of the peafants in Poland, that nothing can exceed the eager-

nefs

4

nefs with which they all fly from the scene of their flavery the moment their mafters are driven away. Thefe are the effects of that tyranny which all the Polifh nobility exert upon their vaffals; fo that in cafe the Ruffians fhould reftore thefe numerous provinces, the Poles will return to deferts, inftead of well-peopled eftates.

The 16th I got to Obloka; the diftance forty-fix miles; ftill in the province of Mif-law. All this track is a fine rich country, but very poorly peopled, many villages being deferted. I paffed a very large feat, belonging to a Polifh nobleman, in ruins. Whoever de-clares againft the Ruffian party, are fure to have their eftates laid wafte, and many of their peafants carried off; and in the pro-vinces which lie near to the frontiers of that empire, they are driven away, and every thing feized by the enemy. There are not many finer countries than great part of this province, but it is in a defolate ftate. I have met with no parties of Poles, nor any appear-ance of war: the Emprefs has a quiet and effectual poffeffion of much the greateft part of Lithuania; and fuch parts are the only ones in the kingdom that enjoy any repofe.

The 17th I reached Whitepfki, the capital town of a large province, alfo in the hands of

the

the Ruffians. The country is very woody. In fifty miles, which were this day's journey, near thirty were through a continual foreft; the reft is tolerably well cultivated, and peopled; it is in poffeffion of fome Poles, who fecured themfelves from the beginning by declaring for the Ruffian caufe. They cultivate their own eftates by means of their vaffals, who have fmall cottages, with little plots of ground round them, in which they raife what is neceffary for the fubfiftence of themfelves and their families in three days of the week, which are allowed them, and the reft of the time they work for their lord, under the direction of overfeers. One of thefe noblemen cultivates in this manner above fix thoufand acres of land: his eftate contains above twenty thoufand acres, but much of it is marfh and foreft. This is a reprefentation of all the eftates in Poland in time of peace. The owners of them, however fmall, are all Polifh gentlemen, and entirely equal; but the numerous diftractions they have had from the beginning of their monarchy, have confolidated moft of the fmall properties, fo that at prefent the kingdom is generally divided into large eftates. Every owner cultivates his land by means of the peafants on it, who belong to him as much as the trees which
grow

grow on the foil; thus the Poles are the greateft farmers in the world, for fome of their princes poffefs whole provinces, containing feveral hundred thoufand acres of land, and all their revenue, which is very confiderable, is raifed by this cultivation. The principal value of eftates is the vicinity to a navigable river; for without this advantage they have not a vent for the immenfe quantity of corn which they raife. The ftubbles I faw upon the eftate juft now mentioned, were of all the common forts, and very extenfive, wheat, barley, oats, peafe, beans, buck-wheat. I faw a few turneps, but the quantity did not feem to be any thing proportioned to the extent of corn.

In the night of the 17th the weather changed, which had hitherto favoured me fo remarkably; very heavy rains fell with fleet and fnow, and continued fo bad the next day, that I ftaid at Whitepfki that day and the two following ones, in expectation of a froft fetting in, for they told me I fhould find the roads much worfe and more liable to be damaged than thofe I had paffed. I ftaid till the 20th, a very fharp froft having fet in for four and twenty hours. The 21ft I reached Goreflaw, through fifty miles of foreft; the 22d I got to Sitefky, the diftance forty three miles; the ground hard frozen, and very good travelling,

velling, but the froft continues and the weather is fharp; this line of country, like the laft, is foreft. The 23d I reached Willifluki, which is in the boundary of Ruffia; but going from one country to the other makes no perceptible difference in the people, manners, or language; which is a circumftance that threatens the Poles not a little. I paffed through another colony of emigrants from that kingdom, who are feated on an eftate of the emprefs's, which came to her not long fince by forfeiture; it contains about four and twenty thoufand acres of land, and did not yield the late owner more than feven hundred pounds a year; but the Czarina will prefently make it twice as many thoufands, for there is the fineft timber for mafts on it that is to be found in all this country; and fhe is making a fmall ftream, that leads to the Iwanna, navigable; the expence will be but little; and fhe will carry her timber then to Petersburg by water, which will prove a moft important acquifition. The Polifh fettlement contains three hundred and forty farms, each a family; they had exactly the fame terms as thofe I gave an account of before. They are feated in a plain thinly fcattered with trees, which they have cleared away: the foil I was informed, for I could not

not fee it, is very deep and rich: they have each fifty acres divided by the Emprefs; and they have made many interior divifions. I was told that in Poland there are fcarcely any in-clofures, but the Emprefs takes care that all the newly cultivated tracks in her dominions fhall be inclofed, being informed that they were the principal caufes which have fo much advanced the husbandry of England ; and it is remarkable that the Poles fall very readily into it, and divide their fifty acres into feve-ral fields, as if they perfectly well underftood the importance of the conduct. They culti-vate wheat, rye, oats, peafe, beans, and buckwheat; and have many crops of Swe-difh turneps for the winter fupport of their cattle ; they get two quarters of wheat and rye from an acre, but fometimes lefs ; three of oats; and four of beans : and they reckon that an acre of turneps will winter two cows. It will be a prodigious advantage to this co-lony, the cutting a canal for the conveyance of the timber to Petersburg, for their products will find the fame way to a moft advantageous market. All thefe people are perfectly happy and contented ; they are not deceived; on the contrary, they find their fituation to the full as good as they were made to expect; and they

all fpeak of the Emprefs in the higheft terms
of admiration and gratitude.

This fyftem of peopling her dominions is
certainly the greateft exertion of politicks that
fhe could poffibly have fhewn : other princes
have been willing to increafe the number of
their fubjects, by affording a refuge to emigrants in their dominions, but nothing elfe ;
whereas the Emprefs is at a confiderable expence in planting them in hers ; fhe fpares
no coft to make the number as great as poffible ; although from the cheapnefs of the
country, it is done at, comparatively fpeaking,
a fmall expence, yet when fuch numbers as
fhe has thus received and fettled are taken into
the account, the fum of money annually expended in this truly noble way, will be found
by no means fmall.

The 24th I reached Opolzko, the diftance
above forty miles ; part of the country is
foreft, and part of it a level plain, or extended meadow, which did not feem to be
marfhy. I paffed feveral villages, which
feemed well peopled ; and much of the country is tolerably cultivated. Opolzko is a fortified town, and ftands in the middle of a fmall
foreft on a very pretty river ; it is not large,
but well built confidering it is in Ruffia, where
fcarcely any thing is ever ufed but timber,

of

of which there is great plenty all over the empire.   The 25th it fnowed inceffantly, and fo
hard, that I was forced to ftop till the 27th,
before I could proceed on my journey ; that
is, till the fnow which laid thick on the
ground was frozen ; and then I was provided
with fledges, which are a very eafy, expeditious, and agreeable way of travelling ; and
pleafed me fo exceedingly, that I wifhed for
a longer journey on the fnow than I now had
to travel ; the cold was not fo penetrating as I
expected to find it.

From Opolzko to Peterfburg, is two hundred and feventy miles, which I travelled
in four days with great eafe.   And here
ends this route through the weftern provinces of this great empire; which are the fineft
and moft populous in it; for tho' I have been
informed that Siberia, and other immenfe
regions to the eaft, confift of as fertile a foil
as any in the world, and fome parts of them
feated in as mild a climate, yet the near neighbourhood of the roving Tartars, in the fouthern and fineft tracks, renders them almoft continued defarts : Ruffia, it is true, has conquered many of them fo completely, that they
are not only tributary, but alfo entirely unable to exert themfelves againft the empire,
nationally fpeaking ; but with individuals the

cafe

cafe is different, and thofe provinces could not
be fettled, without thefe Tartar neighbours
being driven entirely away, or extirpated:
fo that the weftern provinces which are near
to trade, and to the feat of government, are thofe
of much the greateft importance : through
thefe I have travelled above two thoufand
miles, fo that I am able to form a pretty accurate general idea of the country.

It appears upon the whole, to be much
better peopled than I expected to find it. It
is true there are many forefts in which you
may travel a whole day without feeing any
habitations ; and in other parts of the empire,
to a much greater extent ; but we are not to
look in Ruffia for the population of the moft
weftern countries of Europe ; if fuch was to
be found, this empire, which is of a much
greater extent than that of the Romans, would
be as powerful alfo ; but the common ideas
of this country being all a defart, are carried
too far : It is very badly peopled, taking the
whole together ; but many of the provinces
through which I paffed are very populous : the
towns are confiderable, and the villages very
thick ; much of the territory in a good ftate
of culture ; and the appearance of it in many
parts flourifhing : to this may be added the
great increafe of people conftantly gaining, by
the

the reception and encouragement given to foreigners to settle, who flock hither in whole troops: I shall not assert that Russia is a populous well cultivated country; all I say is, that there are more parts of it so than I had reason to expect from the accounts I had received, and the books I had read: the latter indeed must necessarily be far from the present truth in most particulars, from the changes that are constantly making, and from the improvements of all kinds which the present Empress so nobly patronizes: and I may venture to predict, that if she enjoys a long life, she will change the face of the whole dominion; all the western provinces will be fully peopled: wherever the soil is fit for cultivation—the crown lands will be brought to yield a very great revenue, and general improvement spread around.

Upon my arrival at Petersburg I hired my old lodgings which had been empty since I left them: I was not determined what course to take; business wanted me much in England, for I had received letters from three tenants in Northamptonshire, complaining of my agent; and counter ones from my agent, complaining of my tenants; in which case, nothing is effectual but a landlord's presence; on the contrary, the season was so advanced, that it was impossible to go by sea; and journeys in the

depth

depth of winter are to me extremely difagreeable, and the more fo, fince habit had made
me attentive to the ftate of all the countries I
paffed through, and inquifitive in examining
the agriculture of them; which is very badly
performed in the midft of fnows: this made
me think of fpending the winter at Peterfburg,
and taking my way home in the fpring, either
through Poland and Germany, or by the way
of Turkey to the Adriatic, and fo to Italy; but
not relifhing the idea of a winter, in latitude
60, I did not determine.

In this fufpence I fpent a fortnight, which
time I paffed very agreeably, by means of a
more extended acquaintance than I had made
before; and I was particularly happy in Mr.
Mafon's arrival at Peterfburg, who had travelled quite acrofs Poland from Vienna; he
defigned to take advantage of the fnow, to
travel through Siberia, a defign I much dif-
fuaded him from: however, he determined
on refting himfelf a month at Peterfburg; and
my being fo fortunate as to have much of this
gentleman's company at my quarters, made
the time and the feafon pafs away very agreeably: we converfed together upon the mutual
fubject of our travels, which proved to me a
fund of inexhauftible pleafure; for Mr. Mafon, befides croffing Poland, had been all over
Germany—

Germany—through part of Hungary; over Italy, France and Spain. He had been long upon this tour, and has contracted fuch a habit of moving about, that I believe he will not fettle again, till he has travelled all the world over : Laft winter he fpent on the coaft of Africa, and he has determined, for the fake of feeing the furprizing change, to pafs this in the ice and fnows of the north. This, it muft be confeffed, is feeing and becoming acquainted with human nature in every form, and with all the cuftoms of the world; and to a perfon who has an inclination for fuch a way of life, which is ftrong in my friend Mr. Mafon, it is purfuing the inclination effectually.

A perfon who lives genteely at Petersburg, efpecially if he be a foreigner, is fure to get eafily into the beft company in the court; I had not been fix weeks fettled in my winter habitation, before I had more company than I cared for; but it was not difficult to felect from among them, fome whofe converfation was equally agreeable and inftructive. And I never fpent my time in a manner that was more to my inclination, than in the company of Mr. Mafon, M. de Reverfholt a general officer in the Ruffian fervice, a native of Saxony; the baron Minchewfe a Ruffian

nobleman,

nobleman, and the count de Selliern, a nobleman fettled in Ruffia, but of Polifh extrac-
tion.   Thefe men are perfectly well acquainted
with the languages, courts, and armies of the
principal nations in Europe.   They have all
travelled; are learned, polite, and of moft
liberal ideas.   For two months we took it by
turns to have a dinner and fupper provided at
our quarters, where all the reft affembled,
and fpent the beft part of the day, and evening:
the circle was fometimes enlarged by fome
of us bringing. a friend, which was chiefly
three noblemen fettled at Peterfburg, who introduced feveral Ruffian and other foreign
officers, who had feen much fervice, and
were polite and underftanding perfons.   In
this company I had the fatisfaction of having
much converfation upon feveral fubjects of
confequence, in which I was defirous of gaining further intelligence ; particularly concerning the ftate of the diftant provinces of the
empire, the views of the court upon the
Black fea, and the prefent condition of the
Turkifh forces.

M. de Reverfholt, who had been in the
laft campaign againft the Ottomans, gave
me the following particulars of the Turks,
which I think may be agreeable to the
reader :—He obferved, " that if ever the Ruffian

empire engaged in a war with a certainty of
fuccefs, it is in the prefent; for the Turkifh
army is perfectly enervated with peace; ten
quiet years doing more mifchief to it in this
refpect, than forty to any other army in Europe : the Janiffaries have the abfolute command of the empire; and their luxury and
riot, in a time of peace, is fuch, being almoft
without difcipline, that they reduce themfelves
to a level with the worft forces in the Turkifh
army. That, befides this evil, another of a
yet worfe tendency is, the equality of the
Grand Seignor's revenues: money in Turkey
is of the fame cheapnefs as in all other countries of Europe, but the taxes of the empire
continue always the fame; fo that the Turkifh
monarch, although he has now the fame revenue as his predeceffors, ftill is beyond comparifon a much poorer prince.   Many authors
have given ftrange accounts that the Turkifh
policy is fqueezing the bafhas, and by that
means raifing a regular revenue; but he obferved, that it is a great miftake to think this
any equivalent for the decline in the value of
money; that now and then the Grand Seignor
fleeces a bafha, and gets a confiderable fum,
but in no refpect to be named with any regular revenue; that the forfeiture of eftates in
Chriftian countries might almoft as well be

fet

fet down for a revenue, as this of the Turks.
He remarked, that the effects which were
within the power of curious perfons to become
informed of, fhewed that the revenue of the
Turkifh empire was fmaller than in former
times : one ftrong inftance was the number of
their troops being lefs, and this by fo confiderable a number as fixty thoufand men.   It
is afferted as a fact, that the Grand Seignor
cannot bring into the field fo many men as
the Ottoman armies confifted of forty years
ago, by fixty thoufand.   Their artillery,
while great improvements have been made
through all the reft of Europe, has declined
confiderably ; it does not confift of fo many
pieces as formerly, nor are the magazines of
ammunition fo well fupplied.   That in addition to this evil, the richeft province of his
empire, which is Egypt, is in a ftate of little
lefs than rebellion ; and the war with Ruffia
bears fo heavy on them, that they dare not
call for a categorical declaration, almoft
knowing that it would denounce nothing but
war.

In oppofition to this picture, he enlarged
upon the ftate of Ruffia, which, inftead of
being a declining, is really a rifing power ;
that the Emprefs's army never was in fo good
order, nor fo numerous as at prefent; that
the

the troops were veterans, and not such
as had, in a hot and luxurious climate,
flept away their time in peace, but frefh from
a vigorous fervice—men who fcarcely knew
what peace was. The fuccefs, continued he,
which we have already had, fhews that there
is a great difference in the principle of this
war from any former one between the two
empires. It was the bufinefs of two or three
campaigns to prepare for the war, and gain a
fituation from which the enemy might be attacked. Our armies fought to infinite difad-
vantage; they had an immenfe march acrofs
defarts to make, in order to get at the enemy;
and, after a campaign, as long a march back
to get at winter quarters : but now the fcene
has been changed; the northern fhore of
the Euxine is gained; conquefts made in
Moldavia and other Turkifh provinces; fo
that the war is pufhed at once into the enemy's country, and winter quarters gained
there, which is precifely the thing that was
always wanting before; and therefore the
poffeffion of it at prefent can hardly fail of
being attended with the moft fortunate confequences. I think it would be no extravagance to predict the fall of the Turkifh empire being not very far off."

The

The Count de Minchewſe was of a different opinion from M. de Reverſholt in ſeveral
converſations on this ſubject; and the arguments he uſed were to the following purport :
——" I cannot contradict, ſaid that nobleman, the fact of our arms having a better
proſpect of ſucceſs in this war than in any
former one; but there are two circumſtances
which appear to me ſufficiently ſtrong to prevent any ſuch brilliant ſucceſs as my friend
mentions. Firſt, by beating the Turks, and
carrying on two or three campaigns, their
army will be daily improved, while no ſucceſs can make ours better than when they
began the war. In every war which the
Ottoman empire or the Houſe of Auſtria have
carried on againſt us, they have improved in
the ſucceſs of their arms from the continuance of the war; their raw, undiſciplined
troops become veterans, and order and cou-
rage introduced among them from experience.
This circumſtance makes a long and protract-
ed war dangerous in itſelf, or at leaſt more
favourable to the enemy than it can be to us.
The revenues alſo of the two empires, though
there is much truth in what has been aſſerted,
ſtill will not bear a compariſon relative to the
conduct of a war. The Grand Seignor can
certainly ſupport great expences longer than
the

the Emprefs; and, what is of much greater
confequence, his fituation will ever make one
ruble go as far as our five; for the Black fea
keeps open a conftant navigation for fupport-
ing their armies directly from their grand
magazine, Conftantinople; and which will
always be of great fervice, though a Ruffian
fleet was upon that fea; but if they were de-
prived of that advantage, yet there is no comparifon between the eafe of recruiting the
Turkifh armies with the beft troops from
their provinces immediately at their backs,
and the immenfe diftance which every thing
from Ruffia has to go before it can arrive at
our army; and this, I think, is almoft fufficient
to prevent any very important fuccefs.   All
thefe points can hardly fail of making a pro-
tracted war more fatal to us, by the greatnefs
of the expence, than it can be to the Turks.
As to making a very bold pufh to finifh the
war in two or three campaigns, by aiming
fpeedily at Conftantinople, there are too many
dangers in the plan to think that any commander would hazard it.   From the two
great frontier fortreffes, Ockzakow and Ben-
der, there are near four hundred miles to
Conftantinople.   The Danube, with its fix
mouths, and vaft marfhes, befides a great line
of fortreffes, all lie in the way; and after that,

near

near three hundred miles of a very defenfible country. Such a march muft, in the nature of the propofition, leave all the provinces to the weft of Moldavia and Wallachia behind; fo that nothing would be eafier than a Turkifh army to be collected in thofe provinces, and to cut off the communication and retreat of the grand army: in fuch a fituation it would be almoft impoffible for it to efcape ruin. The Turks would have nothing to do but to deftroy the country, harrafs its march, and difpute every inch of land, and every poft, ftill avoiding a general engagement: the leaft error in the Ruffian general would be deftruction, and nothing but continued and fignal victories could be crowned with fuccefs. In fuch a fituation, I am not clear that the taking Conftantinople would be decifive. But the war could never be carried on upon this plan; none is feafible but making abfolutely fure of all the country as you advance; to leave nothing behind you unconquered, or unpoffeffed; but to advance flowly, campaign after campaign. If ever we are able to make any impreffion of confequence upon the empire of the Ottomans, it muft certainly be in this method."

This difcourfe I thought carried with it great marks of knowledge, and a very attentive

tive eye to the chances of the prefent war
with the Turks; and I muft again repeat,
what I obferved upon another occafion, that
whenever a perfon, who minutes the obfervations he has made in his travels, has the fatisfaction of meeting with perfons thus capable
of yielding inftruction, it may be as ufeful to
take notes of their opinions as of his own;
and accordingly I have feldom failed doing it.
Upon revifion, I am inclined to own, that
fuch parts of my memorandums have greater
value than I fhould have been able to have given
them.——I afked the baron, if he did not
think that events of great importance might
attend a victorious Ruffian fleet in the Euxine?
He replied, I do not fee that events, fuch as
we have been fpeaking of, can ever arife
from it, except in one cafe; and the poffibi-
lity or probability of that muft depend on circumftances, of which we are all ignorant till
they are tried.   In making a conqueft of the
Crim, or of the provinces to the north of the
Danube, and to awe and curb the Tartars in
the Turkifh alliance; in all thefe cafes, a victorious fleet would be of infinite importance,
and give advantages to our arms which no
other circumftances could.   But I do not apprehend it poffible for any fleet to force its
way through the Streights, and attack Con-
6   ftantinople

ftantinople by water. But if the fleet on the
Black fea was numerous enough to take on
board the whole Ruffian army, with all its
camp, baggage, artillery, provifions, &c. I
know not whether it would not be poffible to
land them within two or three days march
of Conftantinople; nay, in cafe the coaft is favourable to difembarking, in one day's march.
In this cafe, the expedition would not be in
the abfolute danger of mifcarrying from a
march of four hundred miles, with a certainty
of the retreat being cut off, but the event
thrown at once on that of a battle, in a fituation where a victory, fupported and maintained
by fuch a fleet, would probably overthrow
the empire; for there is a wide difference between gaining fuch a victory frefh from the
fhips, and fo fupported, and the fame fuccefs
without any fupport, and after the repeated
and certain loffes of a long and defperate
march. But to fuch a fcheme there would
be many objections, though not fo ftrong as
to the other: the greateft would be the difficulty of procuring, manning, and fup-
porting fuch a fleet as would be neceffary to
make the conduct at all fecure; and this is fo
great, that it would never be poffible to effect,
in confequence of events that fell out after a
war began; for many years would be neceffary

fary for the mere building fuch a fleet, and
great treafures muft be expended in it. It
could never therefore be executed without
the idea being conceived in a time of peace,
and the fleet built in confequence, and ready
for ufe, with fkilful mariners and pilots ready
at the breaking out of the war : which ftate
of the cafe fuppofes the Emprefs to be in poffeffion of all the north coaft of that fea, and
to have the free navigation of it; for without both, it would be impoffible to think of
the execution of fuch a plan. Thus you fee
what long preparation muft in any cafe be
neceffary to form a confiftent plan for attacking Conftantinople; and yet I am perfuaded
that this is the only plan that can ever prove
fuccefsful. Firft, there muft be a war, and
a fuccefsful one; for fuch muft be that which
gives poffeffion of Little Tartary and the
Crim to the Emprefs. After this war,
no time fhould be loft in raifing a naval
force upon the Black fea, fuperior to any
thing the Turks can fit out. Thirdly, that
fea muft be moft minutely navigated, that
every fhip may have a pilot who knows the
rocks, banks, currents, &c. And laftly, a
fucceeding war muft happen fo fuccefsful, as
to put us in poffeffion of the provinces north
of the Danube; for even by fea it might be

fatal to make the attempt with a ftrong enemy left behind fo near as Ockzakow, Ben-der, or any places in that country.—When all thefe previous fteps were taken, and had proved fuccefsful, then I fhould fuppofe the attempt might be made, and with a proba-bility of fuccefs. I do not fpeak of the prac-ticability of landing on the fouth-weft coaft of the Euxine, becaufe I have been often told that it is all a very fafe coaft, and proper for landing on."

The whole month of December, and the beginning of January 1770, we fpent in our mutual vifits at Peterfburg; and I may fay with great truth, and without paying the o-ther members a compliment, that I never paffed any time more agreeably : now and then Mr. Mafon and myfelf appeared at court, which is neceffary here ; and the Emprefs learning that we were great travellers, entered more than once into converfation with us ; and enquired into our opinions of feveral ob-jects we had viewed. She is referved in the manner of her fpeech, but has a noble open countenance, with a becoming greatnefs in her air and carriage. There is nothing lively or pleafing at court, the whole being but a dull tho' a fine fcene. It is certain that the great wifdom which has hitherto appeared

in

in all the actions and councils of this princefs, flows from her own perfonal genius and abilities : I have not learned that fhe has any minifters, whofe diftinguifhed parts would give one any reafon to fuppofe the fuccefs owing to them; befides, it is well known here, that the Emprefs is very determinate in her opinion. She afks and hears the advice of her council upon important affairs; but fhe generally follows her own opinion, which is evident from her acting directly contrary to the opinion of the whole in two or three affairs of confequence; and in which the fuccefs that followed, proved clearly that her own judgment was better than that of all her minifters. She is remarkable for being exceeding quick in her decifions; fhe never acts from long and repeated confideration, but determines almoft inftantaneoufly, and executes with equal celerity. Such a difpofition is certainly fitter for the conduct of great affairs, than one in which more caution, and a greater degree of prudence appeared; for nothing is fo fatal in the government of an empire, as inconftancy and irrefolution. He who confiders long before he determines, muft infallibly mifs many opportunities, which to more active minds are feized the inftant they appear.

The

The laſt week in January, Mr. Maſon informed me that he had determined on an excurſion into Siberia on the ſnow, and attempted
to perſuade me to accompany him ; I did not
like the ſcheme, as it muſt prove a long and
tedious journey; and in my turn, I propoſed an
excurſion wherever he pleaſed for a month,
which would give us both an opportunity of
ſeeing the nature of this travelling ; we con-
verſed often upon this ſubject before we could
decide ; as we preſently determined to break
the length of the winter, by ſome excurſion
of this ſort. I expatiated to him upon the
drearineſs of ſo long a journey upon the ſnow,
and offered to accompany him to Iſpaham, in
Perſia ; which was moving into a warm climate, inſtead of freezing on the ſnows of the
north ; beſides, ſuch a plan would ſhew us
a country highly worthy of our attention, and
introduce us into quite a new ſcene. He ob-
jected to taking ſuch a journey in the depth
of winter, aſſerting, and truly, that to have
it agreeable, it ſhould be made in the ſpring.
At laſt he came into the ſcheme of a ſhort
excurſion ; and that we might have the ſnow
in perfection, he determined to point full
north, and viſit Archangel, and the coaſt of
the White ſea.

As

As this journey was more a fcheme of a-
mufement than obfervation; and as it was performed while the ground was covered feveral
feet deep with frozen fnow, it afforded very
little matter that is worthy of regiftering in
this journal. We croffed the lake of Ladoga,
upon the ice and fnow to Oloucky, thence
crofs the lake Onega to Cargapol, and from
thence through a great foreft to Archangel.
The diftance is about three hundred miles,
which took us only five days; we ftopped for
lodgings at the towns we paffed; and the
fcenery of the country, which exhibited a
world of fnow in every phantaftic form that
can be imagined, was a fource of perpetual
amufement. The weather was very fevere;
but it is incredible how warm a compleat fuit
of fur, well furrounded with cloaks of the
fame, keeps one; I believe I could have flept
all night upon the fnow, and full in the
keeneft wind, without any other covering
than my furs; but travelling in cold countries has made me hardy; Mr. Mafon often
complained, when I felt not the leaft incon-
venience. The fmooth and immenfe plain
formed on the two lakes, is an object amazingly ftriking; and the vaft forefts rifing out
of the fnow in fome places, and in others covered with it, exhibited fcenes infinitely mag-

P 3   nificent

nificent. I had many opportunities of feeing
the winter life of the peafants, the inhabitants of lonely cottages in the midft of thefe
unbounded fnowy regions. They lay in a
ftore for winter of falted meat indifcriminate-
ly of whatever fort they have ; alfo a quantity
of rye, barley, peafe or meal ; and they lay
up likewife, a confiderable portion of dried
fifh, which they cure in the fmoak of their
cabbins : this winter ftock, with the fowls
and accidental beafts they kill in ranging the
forefts, fupply them tolerably well. They
cloath themfelves very warm in the fkins of
ordinary forts of beafts, that hardly deferves
the name of furs : and the plenty of wood
every where to be found, makes firing fo
cheap an article to them, that their winter
lives I take to be much more comfortable than
their fummer ones ; for their lords have not
fo much work for them to perform, fo that
more of their time is their own ; the greateft
regale that can be given them is that of a
dram ; and we have often found, that they
would in any little contraƈt perform much
more than they agree to, if a dram is added.
This in fo cold a country, and where the articles of luxury among the poor are fo extremely limited, is not to be wonder'd at.

Archangel

Archangel is a fmall town, almoft on the mouth of the Divini, which river is very broad, and deep, and forms an excellent harbour. It contains about five thoufand inhabitants, but the number once was near thirty thoufand, when it was the great ftaple of all the trade which the Englifh and Dutch carried on with Ruffia, before Peter the great founded Peterfburg. It is worthy of obfervation, that from that port there was a confiderable export of Ruffian commodities, particularly naval ftores and furs, before that great commerce was in being, which has fince arofe at Peterfburg. In thofe days it was not an uncommon thing to fee three or four hundred fail of fhips at a time in this harbour, but now very few refort there: It is a poor place; the buildings containing nothing that is at all worthy of notice: They have a cathedral, and an archbifhop of the Greek church; but every thing looks much on the decline.

To avoid returning to Peterfburg by the fame road we had come, Mr. Mafon propofed our croffing the White fea on the ice, and taking a fmall compafs through Lapland, and turning fouthwards round that fea down to the lake Ladoga, and fo home to Peterfburg: this plan I readily agreed to, and accordingly we executed it. From the promontory of

P 4   Catfnoze,

Catfnoze, acrofs to Parfiga in Lapland, is about feven and thirty miles, which we paffed in lefs than a day, though not without fome danger. From thence we went to Pohina, then to Kola, almoft on the north fea, and turning fouth to Keretta, paffed out of Lapland from Kovoda, into Carelia, having travelled near five hundred miles through Mufcovite Lapland. I expected to find nine tenths of the country a defart; but it is not fo; on the contrary there are feveral little towns, and among thofe on the coaft there is a fmall trade divided; a fhip on a coafting voyage now and then comes in fummer, to purchafe furs with fuch commodities as are moft in requeft among the Laplanders. There is very little cultivation among them; but they have large orchards, which furnifh them with an ordinary fort of apple: what corn they fow, is chiefly rye, and a little barley; and this is a new thing, for formerly they lived entirely upon hunting and fifhing, which are at prefent their principal dependance; they dry both flefh and fifh for winter provifion, and feem not much to regard the feverities of the climate. I do not enter into any particular defcription of them, or their manners, becaufe I find that the accounts which I have read are very juft. The face of the country,

from

from what could be feen of it in this feafon,
cannot be difagreeable; it confifts of many
open plains, gentle hills, and woods; fome
of which are open groves, having no under-
wood in them.   This province pays the Emprefs but one tax, which is a certain tribute
of furs; the amount of which is confiderable.
The rental of the eftates, which are fituated
in it, is paid entirely in furs and fkins, for
which the peafants have liberty to cultivate
whatever land they want, and alfo to hunt and
fifh on all the eftates.   In fuch a country it may
be fuppofed, that large tracks of land yield
but very fmall returns; I was affured afterwards by a gentleman at Peterfburg, that he
has a track of fixty miles long, by four and
twenty broad in fome places, and the income
of it was not four hundred pounds a year neat
at Peterfburg.

Upon our return to that city, we renewed our
former fociety in order to pafs the reft of the
winter in as agreeable a manner as poffible;
a purpofe, which I found was fortunately anfwered, and made me often reflect with pleafure on my determining to winter here.   But
I believe, much in fuch cafes is to be attributed to one's determining beforehand to make
the beft of all thofe inconveniencies which
may be occafioned by difference of climate or
seafon.

feafon. In the depth of winter the inhabitants of Ruffia keep chiefly within doors; the fociety of the fire-fide is then the only refuge from the inclemency of the weather: this naturally begets a more fociable temper; and a greater willingnefs to be pleafed, than if all common objects divided the attention and occupied one's hopes and fears. Whether this is or is not a rational account of the matter, I have however often experienced the cafe; and tho' my acquaintance this winter at Peterfburg wanted no circumftances to fet them off, yet I think I enjoyed their converfation more, than if it had been in the midft of the mildnefs of a winter in Andalufia.

The count de Sellirne informed us the middle of March, that he fhould very early in the fpring repair by the Emprefs's order to Azoph, to make the campaign which was meditated againft the Turks in Georgia; and in which he expected a commiffion of importance. This turned our converfation for feveral days on the views of the court of Ruffia, in the war in that part of the world; and the Baron Minchewfe afferted, that attacking the Turks in their provinces, between the Black fea and the Euxine, was one of the wifeft meafures that could be adopted, and the beft calculated of any to give a great diverfion to

their

their arms, to the eafe of the war in the
provinces on the north of the Danube. It is
a territory of very great importance, from its
fituation between the two feas, as well as from
the finenefs of the climate and the fertility of
much of the foil. It is by means of thefe
provinces that they hold fo great a command
of the Black fea, entirely furrounding it by
their dominions and ports. By thefe provinces alfo, the communication is kept up
between their other dominions, and the Tartars in fubjection or alliance with them, after
the Ruffian army cuts it off on the weftern
coaft. Such a diverfion, if made by an army
tolerably powerful, would have great effects;
thofe eaftern provinces are weak, drained of
their troops, and the fortreffes never in good
order ; if all the maritime ones were attacked
one after another by an army in concert
with a fleet, the war might in two campaigns
be carried to the fouthern coaft of that fea,
which would alarm the Turks exceedingly,
and occafion great drafts from their grand
army.

Upon another occafion, when we were
converfing upon the profpects of the prefent
war, I related the journey I had made from
the Ukraine along the frontiers of Poland to
Peterfburg; and obferved, that an immenfe

track

track of country was not only in the hands of
the Ruffian troops, but the towns and villages
partly peopled with Ruffians, while the old
inhabitants were all flying into Ruffia: this,
I remarked, had all the appearance of the Emprefs's defigning to annex thofe countries to her
dominions. The Count faid, in reply, that
there were feveral provinces in Lithuania
which the ancient Czars had long claimed;
they were once independent; and after putting themfelves firft under the protection of
Poland, then under that of Ruffia, and then
going back to Poland again, difputes about
the fovereignty had happened, which extended in fome degree to the whole grand duchy
of Lithuania: he therefore fuppofed the Emprefs might keep thofe provinces in her
hands, if not retain them, at leaft for making
a divifion with the republick, and afcertaining
clearly the boundary, if ever a time of tranquillity fhould return. He faid that there was
great reafon to believe fo very political a
princefs would not miftake fo much, as to
form any confiderable conquefts from Poland,
and that for two unanfwerable reafons: firft,
becaufe they are not to her worth having,
after the inhabitants are all fwept away; by
her encouragements fhe attracts the greater
part, and fear fends away the reft: if, on a
peace,

peace, the owners of thofe provinces are at the
trouble to re-people them from other parts of
Poland, they will only be at work for her, as
in a future rupture the fame game will be
played over again, and the Emprefs gain every
thing fhe wants, which is not territory, but
people. The fecond reafon is no lefs forci-
ble; if fhe was to difmember any provinces
of confequence from the kingdom of Poland,
fhe would fcarcely fail of bringing the united
arms of Auftria and Pruffia on her; neither of
which powers can ever fee, with any degree
of fatisfaction, the increafe of this empire's
greatnefs, and would declare againft it the
inftant any appearance took place of making acquifitions from Poland, which to them
would carry appearances of greater defigns;
and if Poland fell into the hands of any neigh-
bour, the ballance of power in all this part
of the world is at once deftroyed; and of all
events, none can be more againft the interefts
of Auftria and Pruffia, than to bring the
Ruffian power nearer to them than it is at
prefent. Peopling her waftes is the great object of the Czarina; Polifh provinces would
be of no value to her; if territory is her object, it cannot be in Poland, but on the
Euxine fea, where it would bring trade, and
a command with it, of much more confe-

6

quence to her than half of Poland. The Ruffians you faw fettling on the frontier provinces, muſt be merely fuch as are attracted
by the armies with a view of fupplying them,
at a time when the deferted houſes and farms
of the Poles were ready to receive them ; but
they will all be glad to return when the occaſion
of their going is removed. Thoſe provinces
are now under the civil as well as military ad-
miniſtration of Ruſſia, which muſt of confequence carry a great number of Ruſſians there,
whoſe reſidence can be no longer than the occaſion continues. All will return upon a general pacification.

I ſhould think, in good politics, the Count's
opinion muſt be right ; and that the Empreſs
keeps poſſeſſion of ſo many Poliſh provinces,
in order to be better able to carry off all the
inhabitants ; which is certainly making the
beſt uſe of them that can be to her. But,
at the ſame time, ſhe acquires all that ſtrength
which would be the confequence of ſeizing
the provinces themſelves ; and therefore her
rivals, who would declare againſt her for one,
ſhould, to be confiſtent, do the ſame for the
other ; for there certainly can be no doubt but
the increaſe of a million of ſubjects, fixed on
the crown lands of this empire, would
ſtrengthen the monarch on the throne far
more

more than the acquifition of a Polifh province, containing a million, and yield four
or five times the wealth.

The approach of the fpring made Mr.
Mafon and myfelf think of leaving Peterfburg.
He determined to travel into Perfia, and, if
the country is tolerably fettled, to go by land
through the Mogul's empire to our fettlements
on the coaft of Coromandel; an idea very
worthy of a man who, I believe, will never
ceafe to travel till he ceafes to live. But as I
have no defire to pafs away my life without
the fatisfaction of fixing, I fhall bend my
courfe homewards, with the pleafing idea of
turning a country farmer in Northampton-
fhire, and putting in practice, on my own
eftate, fome of the various cultures and methods which I have viewed in fo many
places.

The 3d of April, 1770, I left Peterfburg,
taking with me five attendants to conduct me
fafe through Poland; among whom were
two foldiers, who could fpeak German and
Polifh: of the former language I have enough
to underftand common converfation. Such a
retinue in England would coft a traveller four
or five pounds a day; but I could travel in
Ruffia or Poland for four and thirty fhillings
a day, all expences included, except extraor-

6   dinary

dinary ones : when I ſtop at large towns,
the landlords, though they are very reaſona-
ble, will yet ſwell the account higher than
that.   I arrived the 5th at Narva, which is
one hundred miles ; the country very badly
inhabited, but much of it cultivated.   The
froſt is beginning to go ; ſo in ten days or a
fortnight we may expeＣt ſummer, which, in
the northern climates, comes at once, without the intervention of ſpring.   The ſnow
melts apace ; till it is quite gone, the roads
will be bad ; but I have even, in their preſent circumſtances, travelled on worſe.

Narva is prettily ſituated on the banks of a
fine river, though not a deep one, as ſhips of
any ſize cannot come up to the town : it is
well built, and ſtrongly fortified.   Here is a
conſiderable trade in hemp, flax, timber, pot-
aſhes, and moſt of the commodities which
are exported from Peterſburg.   Almoſt all the
trade is in the hands of the Engliſh and
Dutch ; but the former are much the greateſt
purchaſers : the trade which the latter carry
on here has long been on the decline.   I left
Narva the 6th, at noon, and taking the banks
of the river, followed it two days, when I arrived
at Salatſki, which is above ninety miles from
Narva, ſtanding at the bottom of a very fine
lake, above forty miles broad, and as much
long.

long.   All this country is pretty well cultivated.   I faw many fields of rye beautifully
green, though fo lately covered with fnow,
and much of them now under it.   The 8th I
reached Plefcow, on a lake of the fame name,
fome parts of which, from the wooded iflands
which are thick in it, are very beautiful.   All
this country is as well cultivated as any part
of Ruffia.   It produces a large quantity of
flax ; but they reckon the foil rather too light
for hemp.   They have two feafons for fowing both wheat and rye ; October, and April
and May; but they reckon that the former
feafon yields the beft produce.   They grow
much more corn than is neceffary for their
own confumption, which, with their flax, is
exported by the port of Narva; water carriage
giving them that opportunity at a very cheap
rate.   Wheat yields here two quarters, and
fometimes more, upon an acre ; rye not more
than wheat : barley is not fown till the middle of May, but the heat of the fun brings an
early harveft ; it is not reckoned a very profitable grain here; they get from two quarters to two and an half per acre : oats yield
three and an half.   I had been informed, that
in Livonia, one method of cultivation was
very extraordinary, which was, that of flood-
ing vales that would admit it, and keeping

them as fifh-ponds for three or four years,
and then, letting the water off, they cultivate
it for corn for five or fix years; after which
the water muft be let on again to fertilize it
afrefh : but on enquiry I found it was not in
this part of the country : but they ufe here
almoft as many wood afhes for manuring their
lands as they do in Sweden, and fay that no
other manure has fo great an effect.

The roads growing but indifferent, I did
not reach Marienburg till the 10th; the diftance better than fifty miles. The country is
woody in parts, but much of it very well cultivated. I paffed through large tracks of
young wheat and rye, which looked extremely well; and the peafants were all bufy in the
fields with their ploughs, which they work,
fome with horfes, and fome with oxen. They
were tilling their lands for barley and oats,
and alfo flax; for the latter of which they ap-
propriate their beft foils, if not wet clays; but
they prefer a fine light fandy loam for it.
An acre of good flax is worth from three to
five pounds; but they raife much that does
not yield three. Marienburg is a fmall town,
tolerably well built, and moft romantically
fituated on a promontory of land which pro-
jects into a large lake; fo that it is joined to
the main land only by a narrow neck, not
much

much wider than the road. An inland place in a country not full of manufactures, can scarcely be of any great importance. Marienburg was once of consequence for its strength, and the scene of several military expeditions, when belonging to the Teutonic knights. It is at present poor, but strong for this part of the world. The people live cheaply, from the fertility of the neighbouring country, and the vast quantity of fish which they get out of the lake. The farmers manure their land around the lake with a kind of ouze, which they dig up on the banks of it : it is of a deep blue colour, about two feet deep, cuts like wet peat, and is composed of rotten vegetables ; for there is an immense growth of weeds every year in the lake, which drive ashore and rot, and, with a mixture of mud, forms this manure, which is of the nature of marle, and fertilizes their fields for many years. I have no doubt but the same materials might be found on the coasts of many other lakes ; but custom not having made the use of them common, the husbandmen neglect them.

The 11th I got to Pebalgen, another town built on a lake ; the distance about forty miles, through a territory, part good, and part of it marshy ; but all the lands that would admit

2　　　　　　　　　of

of culture, feemed to be under cultivation, and yielded wheat, rye, barley, oats, and pulfe. They alfo cultivate cabbages for the winter food of their herds, which are very numerous. It is a large red cabbage, which ftands the utmoft feverity of the winter, and is taken from under the fnow in full perfection for all forts of cattle, who are wonderfully fond of them. They ufed to fow the Swedifh turnep for this ufe, but come more into the cabbage, from finding the produce much greater. As to its ftanding the winter, from the obfervations I have made, I am inclined to believe the climates in which vegetables fuffer moft, are not thofe where great quantities of fnow fall, but fuch as have fevere frofts without any fnow : the fnow keeps them warm, and greatly protects them from the keen frofty winds, which in other countries cut off fo many vegetables. There is not much flax in this line of country ; but they cultivate a little hemp : however they depend moft upon common hufbandry. It is remarkable that there is a great difference between Livonia, and the other parts of Ruffia which I have been in. The ancient provinces generally are divided into the eftates of the nobility, who cultivate them by means of ftewards and agents, the peafants being all flaves. But

in

in the Ukraine, the land belongs to little freeholders, if I may so call them, who cultivate their own property. Now in Livonia the case differs from both; for here estates are of all sizes, and let out upon farming leases, as in England. There are many seats of country gentlemen, who all have a part of their estates in their own hands; but the peasants, though not so much at their ease as in free countries, yet are not enslaved; they hire large tracks of land, which some of them cultivate extremely well; and many of them are worth considerable sums of money for this part of the world.

The 12th I rode near fifty miles to Cropper, through a country most beautifully watered with small lakes and rivers; it is diversified with gentle hills and groves of fine trees, and great part of it well cultivated; many parts of England have a much worse appearance. The peasants from the general activity seen among them, I take to be a very industrious set of people; scarcely any arable field but what had ploughs at work in it; the soil is sandy, for loams and clays require some time to dry after the snow is gone, before they will admit the cattle to till it; but these lands inclinable to sand are presently dry enough for tillage; they plough variously for their

Q 3   spring

fpring corn, fome only once, others three times. Flax is cultivated by many of them; but they affured me that wheat paid them better, though fome farmers have now and then fuch good flax-crops as induces them to continue the culture. I remarked that moft of them are very attentive through the winter feafon in raifing dunghills, or rather compoft heaps near their houfes; for there was fcarcely a farm without a great fquare heap piled up to a confiderable height; they are compofed of the dung of their cattle, which they winter in houfes, and litter them with rufhes and other aquatic weeds, which they cut up for that purpofe in their numerous lakes and rivers; they alfo add great quantities of mud, alfo wood afhes, &c. and at this time of the year, they mix thefe hills together, turning them over, and incorporating the ingredients; after which they leave them, till they fow barley or plant cabbages, fpreading them on the land before the laft ploughing. This muft all be a very excellent fyftem of hufbandry.

The 13th in the afternoon I reached Riga which is the moft confiderable place for trade next to Peterfburg in the Ruffian dominions. It ftands very advantageoufly for commerce, near the mouth of the river Dwina, which, with its branches extending a great way into

Poland

Poland and Ruffia, bring immenfe quantities of commodities which are exported from this city: Among thefe the principal are hemp, flax, timber for mafts and other purpofes; pitch, tar, and pot afhes; all thefe commodities are produced in the provinces or near them, through which thofe rivers run; and fome of them by means of fhort land carriage from one river to another, much further even from the Ukraine and the Polifh provinces that border upon Turkey. It appears by the regifters of the cuftom-houfe at this town, that more than five hundred fail of fhips, from one hundred and fifty to four hundred tons, have been loaded here in a year; three hundred of which were Dutch, and one hundred and fixty Englifh; but of late the trade of the town has declined, for at prefent there are not many more than four hundred fail cleared outwards, of which about two hundred and forty are Englifh. Every ton of the goods they carry from hence, might be had at our own plantations; but for want of due encouragement we come to Ruffia for them, and pay fome hundred thoufand pounds ballance on the account; which is an inftance of miftaken politicks that never was to be equalled in the annals of the Dutch republick.

Q 4

I had

I had a letter of recommendation to Mr. Scueen, a principal merchant in this town, with whom I fpent the evening; and he not only gave me the heads of the preceding particulars, but I had alfo fome inftructive converfation with him on the prefent ftate of the province of Livonia. Of all Peter the great's conquefts, this was the moft important; being a country which for its products, ports and fituation is of the higheft importance to Ruffia. It forms upon an average, a fquare of 200 miles every way, and contains better than twenty five millions of acres, and near a million of people. Above half the lands he calculates, are under profitable cultivation, either in arable crops or good meadow; and exclufive of woods, marfhes, lakes and rivers. The annual product is about thirteen millions fterling, including timber. Such an eftimate cannot be accurate, I do not give it the reader as a paper of authority; it is nothing more than the calculation of a very ingenious fenfible man, who has many times travelled all over Livonia. The parts which I faw are not equal in culture to others in the province, yet I fhould apprehend that half the track I came through is under culture, meadows included; and as to the number of acres, it is a geographical fact. But I fhould not conceive

3

ceive

ceive there were quite a million of people in
it ; I heard the number once eſtimated at between ſix and ſeven hundred thouſand.   Sup-
poſing ten or twelve millions of acres cultivated, which does not appear to me an exaggerated idea; I do not ſee how the total product
of the province can be eſtimated ſo low as
thirteen millions.   But from this ſketch of
particulars, it is eaſy to conceive that the
importance of the province to Ruſſia is very
great.

Travels

Travels thro' Poland and Pruffia.

CHAPTER VII.

Journey to Dantzick—Defcription of the coun-
try and hufbandry—Trade of Dantzick—
Journey to Warfaw—Miferable ftate of Po-
land—To Brefaw.

THE 14th I left Livonia, and reached
Mittaw, the capital of Courland, the
diftance about eight and forty miles. The
face of the country is exactly the fame as that
of Livonia, and the foil equally fruitful,
which by information I found was the cafe of
the whole dutchy: their products, as hemp,
flax, lintfeed, timber, mafts, pot-afh, fkins,
tar, honey, wax, &c. are confiderable. The
whole country is full of black cattle, and they
have many horfes. Mittaw was in the happy
times of the dukes of Courland, when the
Ketler family had quiet poffeffion, and before
the dutchy and all its towns were ravaged by
the Swedes and Mufcovites, it was then a confiderable and a fine town; it reckoned fifteen
thoufand inhabitants, but now they are not
more than nine thoufand. It is yet an agreeable place, well built with a handfome du-
cal palace, where is fomething of a court with

guards,

guards, and there is always a ſtrong garriſon in it. Of late years there have been great additions to the fortifications. It is now, as well as the whole dutchy, in the hands of the Ruſſians.

From Mittaw, I reached Zagari in Poland on the 15th, being about four and forty miles ; part of the country tolerably cultivated, but not equal to Livonia, or even to Courland ; there were ſome Ruſſian ſoldiers at Zagari to keep the town and the neighbouring country in order, which they do very effectually ; and a great advantage it is to theſe parts of Poland, where the civil war is thus kept under by a foreign power. The advantages of all the cultivation I ſaw are in the hands of the Ruſſians, for the Poliſh nobles through moſt of the great province of Samogitia are driven from their eſtates, and the profits of ſuch of them as are not depopulated all go to the Ruſſians. The cottages of the peaſants are as mean as can well be conceived ; they are chiefly built of turf, and covered with the ſame, being drawn up in a ſpiral form to a point, where is an aperture for the ſmoak to go out ; the room is large enough for the family and the cattle ; all lye together and in the ſame manner. I had read that they uſed in this province none
but

but wooden plough-fhares, through a ridiculous notion that the iron damaged their crops; but this is not true, for I faw many ploughs at work for barley, and all of them had iron fhares, but of a moft aukward conftruction.

The 16th I got to Rofenne, the diftance near fixty miles; through a country that had hardly any appearance of prefent cultivation; many villages I paffed that were deferted, feveral manfions in ruins, and fields entirely wafte that had once been tilled; the whole a very melancholy fpectacle; but much of the country was partly marfh and foreft. The town of Rofenne is a fmall fortified place, which has a Ruffian garrifon; there is an appearance of nothing but poverty in it. The 17th I got to Swingy, a little town about thirty four miles from Rofenne; there is fome land in this line of country under cultivation, being the eftate of a nobleman who enjoys it in tolerable peace under the protection of Ruffia. They fow barley, oats, peafe, beans, and a little rye; I faw feveral ploughs at work; and upon examining them, found that the fhares were wood, to my no fmall furprize; I enquired the reafon of this, and they could give me none, only that they never ufed any other fort; the land here is fandy, and did not

feem

feem to yield good crops : the rye was full of weeds ; I afked if it was to be weeded, and they told me they never weeded any corn at all. The nobleman is an old man, who has his eftate managed in the fame way as his father had; that is, the peafants are miferably oppreffed by his ftewards, and his own income at the fame time contemptible.

The 18th I travelled forty miles to Stocken, all in Pruffia, the country fandy, and not much of it well cultivated, but the peafants are much more at their eafe than in Poland, and this country being fubject to the king of Pruffia, no Ruffians, no Polifh confederacies nor any difturbances happen in it, which is a very great advantage to agriculture; tho' I yet have feen nothing that gives me any great idea of their knowledge in that fcience. This country is much more populous than Samogitia, and the houfes of the peafants built of much better materials. I paffed two or three villages entirely inhabited by Poles who have fled their country, and fettled here by order of the king of Pruffia ; though without any of that noble encouragement I faw exerted in Ruffia; and I believe thofe who take refuge in the latter country, are in other refpects better treated than they are in Pruffia. The 19th I got by dinner to Koningfburg, the diftance

ftance being only twenty miles through a country pretty well cultivated, and tolerably peopled, though the foil is in general fandy, and from its appearance I fhould not apprehend it very good. All the country people were now bufy in preparing their land for fpring fown corn; they plough here with only two cattle in a plough; and I faw fome drawn by a little horfe and a cow; or a little ox; this is very practicable with fo light a foil: they fow large quantities of buckwheat, and reckon it more profitable than barley. Koningfburg is the moft confiderable town which the King has in Pruffia; it is tolerably well fituated, and has a very good harbour with fome trade, but not near equal to that of Riga, though it is a hanfe town. The export is in the fame articles, except hemp and flax, of which the quantity is too inconfiderable to mention. Upon the coaft are found fometimes large quantities of yellow amber, which is to be bought at Koningfburg. The ftreets are broad, but irregular and not well paved; but there are many very good buildings in it, and they reckon above twenty thoufand inhabitants. The King has made feveral attempts to increafe its trade, but they do not feem to be attended with any great effect. Dantzick, on one fide, and Riga on the other, are two fuch

VOL. III.   R   rivals,

rivals, that this place cannot make its trade good againſt them for any thing further than the mere amount of the products of that track of country, which lies nearer to it than to any other.

The 20th I reached Ladſperg, at about forty miles from Koningſburg : the country all ſandy, and, that circumſtance conſidered, pretty well inhabited. Buck-wheat is a great crop with them, I found. They do not ſow it till the end of May : the produce is greater than that of any other grain or pulſe, and the ſtraw they reckon nearly equal to hay for cattle ; an obſervation I had not any where heard of before. The peaſants of this country, I find, are all much freer than in Poland, but they pay very heavy taxes to the King ; yet they are not in ſuch bad circumſtances as the Poliſh peaſants, becauſe taxation is regular ; whereas the payments made by the peaſants to their lords in Poland, are ſo capricious, that they never know when they have paid their total : moſt of it being in cattle, and irregular perſonal ſervices, the beſt liberty that can be given to peaſants is to compound all ſuch for money, which makes their burthens regular, however heavy they may be ; and when this ſyſtem is extended as far as it will go, it in-cludes the tenures of land ; ſo that all the

eſtates

eftates are let on leafe, and the landlord's
whole property pays him a regular intereft in
money : this is the higheft advantage that
can any where be made of the foil—it will
in this cafe always be beft cultivated, and
yield a greater total product than in any other
fyftem, at the fame time that many more
people are maintained than in any other way.
It is not at all neceffary that a country fhould
be free, in order for this fyftem to reign ; it is
as general throughout France, and the arbitrary governments in Italy, as it is in England.
The people, it is true, may be oppreffed ; but
then the oppreffion is different : in France,
the proportion of taxes paid by the farmers
and peafants is quite out of all proportion to
the other claffes of the people ; but then
there is a regularity in their burthens, which
renders them bearable. Taxes upon land,
cattle, crops, or on whatever they may be laid,
muft in their nature have fomething of regularity and proportion in them ; but the perfonal fervice in which the lower ranks of
Poland are kept, is a mere flavery, fuch a
defpotifm as the planters in the Weft-Indies
ufe over their African flaves. Compared
with this, the oppreffed ftate of the Ruffian
peafants is an abfolute freedom ; befides

which,

which, there are many farmers who hire their lands by tenures.

The 21ft carried me about forty miles to Elbing; the country all fandy, yet tolerably well cultivated. It is remarkable that buckwheat, upon thefe fands, very often yields as profitable a produce as wheat on the beft foils : they get five or fix quarters an acre off it ; and the ftraw they reckon excellent food for their cattle in winter. Swedifh turneps they alfo raife to advantage upon them ; and tillage is fo eafy, from the lightnefs of the draught, that they plough their land, after the firft time, with a fingle horfe or cow : but this ploughing with cows is only while they are dry ; they do not ufe them while they give milk. Elbing is, next to Dantzick, the moft confiderable town in Polifh Pruffia : it is a pretty, neat, and well-built place, with a trade that is fufficient to give a brifk circulation of money among the inhabitants : they load many fhips in a year, fometimes above thirty fail, with corn, timber, potatoes, and hides. It is always ftriking, in every little town, to fee the fuperiority that refults from trade : a fmall commerce gives a circulation and a wealth, that diffufes happinefs through every clafs of the people ; the houfes are better built, new ones are erected, and every body

body lives well. But in a country town, fupported by nothing but the agriculture around it, every thing is the contrary; the houfes are poorly built, many are falling into ruin, and all ranks of the people are poor and unhappy. Such are the confequences of bringing commerce into a country, which never fails of giving a new appearance to every object.

The 22d I arrived at the famous city of Dantzick; the diftance about forty miles. I croffed feveral branches of the Viftula, part of the country being within the liberties of the city. This territory, though a poor fandy foil, is moft highly cultivated, and fhews, in every acre, the infinite advantages which refult from liberty and wealth. The burghers have their villas in this territory; and all of them have farms, which they manage in a manner much fuperior to the hufbandry that is to be feen any where elfe in Poland. I faw fome very fine fields of wheat on this apparently barren fand, which I dare fay the moft fertile land in Poland does not exceed: this was owing to manure brought from Dantzick, fuch as dung of all forts, afhes, the fweepings of the ftreets, the offals of the fhops, &c. which being carried out of the city, unto heaps, is fold into the country by the public

R 3 fcavengers;

fcavengers; moft of it is bought by the Dantzickers for their farms; and they raife by this means as fine corn, &c. on their poor fand, as the richeft foils yield that are not equally manured.

Dantzick is a very confiderable city, well fituated on the mouth of the Viftula, with a very advantageous harbour for all but the largeft fhips. It very much refembles Hamburgh, both in the loftinefs of the houfes, the manner of building them, and in the narrownefs of the ftreets. The ftreets and houfes are much cleaner than any others in this part of the world; but neatnefs is not carried to the length it is in Holland. The principal ftreets are planted on each fide in the Dutch way, which is an inftance of ill tafte in the original, which one cannot but be furprifed at ever feeing copied. The city is not large, the circumference not exceeding three miles : it is fortified with a wall, and a double ditch; but the ftrength alone that is its fecurity, is the intereft of all their neighbours that the place fhould continue free : in which circumftance it is in the fame predicament as Hamburgh. Two thoufand regular troops, excellently provided and armed, would be a very weak garrifon ; but they have not feven hundred to fpare, and thofe neither in difcipline,

arms,

arms, or magazines, comparable to the fame number of men in any regular fervice in Europe. In a word, Dantzick has a ftrength to refift nobody but the Poles. They have an arfenal full of ufelefs arms, and talk of poffeffing two or three hundred pieces of cannon; but a great train of artillery may be as infignificant, as are thefe of Dantzick, as a magazine of match-locks.

But the commerce of this city is the object that is alone worth attention; it poffeffing, they reckon, fixteen in twenty parts of all the trade of Poland. This is by means of the river Viftula, and its numerous branches, which fpread through a vaft extent of that kingdom, and are navigable almoft wherever they go. The great article of export is corn, and particularly wheat; they fend off fome years to the amount of five, fix, and feven hundred thoufand pounds; and once the amount arofe to one million two hundred and forty thoufand pounds. Of late years, the quantity is much declined, and, fince the prefent troubles in Poland, has been very trifling; fo that the total, laft year, it was faid, did not amount to one hundred thoufand pounds. All the corn comes in floops and flat-bottomed barges, that carry from thirty to fixty tons, and fome more, and wholly on

account

account of the landlords, who are all nobles
by virtue of their poffeffing lands.   It is raifed
on their eftates by their peafants, who, as I
before obferved, are all flaves ; fo that the Poles
may be faid to farm their whole eftates, whatever be the extent: the barges are their own generally, and the watermen that navigate them
are fome of them their vaffals, and others free-
men, whom they hire in the cities and towns on
the river.   It is fold to merchants at Dantzick,
who lodge it in their granaries, which are
more capacious than thofe of any town in Europe, fome of them eight ftories high.   The
boats bring, befides corn, all the other articles
of fale which the Polifh eftates produce, particularly pot-afh, mafts, plank for fhip-build-
ing, pipe ftaves, which are better than thofe
of Hamburgh, bees-wax in large quantities,
fome hemp and flax, and formerly much of
it manufactured into facking, packing-cloths,
and even linen, but this of late years is much
declined : of all thefe articles, to the amount
of three or four hundred thoufand pounds,
but fometimes not near fo much.   The boats,
on their return, carry back to the nobles,
cities, and towns, all the commodities and
manufactures which they want.   Among
thefe are reckoned, iron from Sweden, of
which they once took two thoufand tons a
year,

year, but the import is fallen to a thousand; East-India goods of all sorts, manufactures of woollen and fine linens, silks, brandy, wines, &c. The Dutch have all the supply of India goods, and most of that of linen and woollen; and the French the principal part of the silks, brandy, wines, and all the West-India commodities. As to England, her trade with Dantzick is very inconsiderable, which is entirely owing to our taking off very few of her commodities: we never pay money for what plank, pot-ash, or hemp we import; and when wheat is so dear in England, that foreign corn is admitted, our merchants have sometimes sent many ships thither to load with wheat, and have paid for their cargoes with our manufactures, of which none are so acceptable in Poland as the hardware goods of Birmingham, Sheffield, Rotherham, &c.

Making use of a letter of recommendation, which I had brought from the Count Selliern, to Mr. Pratsky, a very eminent merchant at Dantzick, and one whose great wealth shews how well he understands the trade of the city, gave me an opportunity not only of getting the preceding particulars upon better authority than I could otherwise have done, but, at the same time enabled me to make some enquiries concerning the present state of Poland, respecting

5 the

the factious views and defigns of the feveral parties which at prefent harrafs that kingdom. I had for three years paft read much concerning them in the public prints of many countries, but could never clearly underftand the real ftate of the kingdom till I travelled from the Ukraine to Peterfburg. The account he gave me was this.

" Poland is divided into two grand parties, the Roman Catholicks, and the Proteftants and Greeks. The former, for fome ages paft, have omitted (as has been the cafe in every country of Europe) no opportunities of oppreffing the latter, and depriving them of that religious liberty to which they have a right by the conftitution of the kingdom. Thefe oppreffions and invafions of privileges begot confederacies of nobles, profeffing the Reformed or Greek religions, who entered into compacts for the defence of their faith, and declaring a full refufal to acknowledge any fovereignty, until their complaints were redreffed. This ftroke was copied immediately in moft parts of the kingdom where thofe religious are found. This gave rife to counter confederacies of the Roman Catholick nobles, with this addition, that they, in their agreement, declared all who did not accede to it to be enemies to the kingdom.

A

A civil war immediately commenced: Ruffian troops, which had long been in the kingdom, were greatly increafed, upon the Emprefs's declaring, in a general manifefto, her protection of the Greek and Reformed religion; and all parts of the kingdom were immediately in arms. In this war, the King, who difliked the whole of thefe proceedings, has been neuter; though it is very well known that the Ruffians are his friends, and that their power preferves him on the throne. The fuccefs of the war at firft was various; but every where the effect of it was deftroying and plundering each other's eftates, and utterly ruining a confiderable part of the kingdom. In the plunder taken on either fide, the peafants are always the moft valuable part: fuch as are not armed by their mafters, but remain at home to cultivate the land, are, upon a fkirmifh or incurfion which proves fuccefsful, carried off and planted upon the victors lands, where they are moft feverely treated, if they do not immediately conform to the religion of their new mafters. Such a fyftem of making war, which has now ravaged Poland three years with great violence, it may eafily be fuppofed, is well enough calculated for reducing the whole kingdom to the condition of a defart. The Ruffians have in

3   general

general been too hard for their enemies, and have cut in pieces a great number of their confederacies as faſt as they are formed; upon which occaſion the counter-reformed Poles enter and utterly deſtroy their eſtates, carrying off the peaſants, and fixing them upon their own lands; and many are ſent into Ruſſia from almoſt every expedition, which, of all the reſt, are thoſe only who have any chance of being fixed out of the reach of conſtant revolutions. This is the preſent ſtate of the kingdom: more than half of it has been laid waſte ſince the war began; and what threatens the whole is, the number of Roman Catholic confederacies, which are formed as faſt as the Ruſſians deſtroy the old ones. Nothing can bring any degree of peace to the kingdom, but the Empreſs increaſing her troops to ſuch a number, as to make a conqueſt of all the Roman Catholic part of the kingdom: and this would give umbrage, it is thought, to other powers, although ſome of them have declared in favour of the Reformed and Greek cauſe—that is, in favour of liberty of conſcience. While the preſent war laſts between Ruſſia and Turkey, the Empreſs cannot ſpare either troops or money for ſuch a plan; but if a peace is concluded with the Porte,

we

we may then look for more decisive meafures."

Upon my afking him his fentiments of the
Ruffian acquifitions, and their keeping poffeffion of fo many provinces, driving away the
Polifh nobility from their eftates, and carrying moft of the peafants into Ruffia; inti-
mating, that I thought the Emprefs had a
fair chance of acquiring fomething important; he replied,—" I do not apprehend that
the Emprefs of Ruffia will think of feizing
any Polifh provinces, becaufe that would
make not only all moderate perfons, and all
well-wifhers to their country among the
Poles, her implacable enemies, but would
deprive her of the ftrongeft pretence fhe has
of interfering, and thereby governing Poland : at the fame time, it would bring her
into a war with Pruffia and Auftria; for neither of thofe powers would fee fuch Ruffian
acquifitions, and fit by quietly. The aims
of that princefs, which I have little doubt are
thofe of a true politician, are to fupport the
party of her own religion, and prevent their
being oppreffed, and to gain fuch a general
power in the kingdom, as to have her will be
treated, in all great national meafures, with
due refpect. Her carrying away the Polifh
peafants to people her crown lands is moft
certainly

certainly a very political conduct; for she
will add thereby equally to her ſtrength and
wealth."

M. Pratſky inſiſted on my taking a dinner
with him, which I did.   He has a large and
convenient houſe, well furniſhed, and much
in the Engliſh manner.   His wife is an agreeable, ſenſible woman, a native of Sileſia,
who talked politicks inceſſantly, and was a
ſtrenuous advocate for the King of Pruſſia.
They had a beautiful young lady, their daugh-
ter, who entertained me on the harpſichord;
Dantzick being pretty well ſupplied with
muſicians from Germany.   M. Pratſky lives
elegantly, but in the German manner, which
is all the taſte there : they ſit long at meals,
and drink very heartily : and among all the
nations that are fond of the pleaſures of the
table, there is always much ſociety, and a
deſire of pleaſing, which does inſtead of the
more refined manners of the ſouthern countries.   Miſs Pratſky, and other ladies I ſaw,
aim in their dreſs, I obſerved, at an imitation
of the French taſte : but I cannot ſay I could
ever admire any imitations, even in dreſs :
whatever nation affects to follow the taſte of
another, will never make any other figure
than that of an halting copyer, who ſhews as
much aukwardneſs as faſhion.   The Engliſh
never

never make fuch fools of themfelves as when they copy the French in their drefs; the two nations are of different genius, and different manners; we never come up to the extravagance of the original; our copy is always tame : go from London to Paris, you are in a new world ; you find what was called French, to be a miferable defective copy of a miferable original.

During my ftay at Dantzick, I was at the Golden Crown, a very good inn lately fitted up and kept by a Dutchman; he charges very reafonably, and fupplied me with good fifh very frefh, and his wines are excellent, particularly old hock.

The 26th I left Dantzick and took the road for Warfaw, in the province of Plofcow : I was informed there were feveral parties of confederates and much fkirmifhing, I therefore took the advantage of travelling with a Dantzick burgomafter, going on publick bufinefs to the King with a company of foldiers for his guard. That day we travelled above forty miles to Kirchow, a fmall town through a fandy track of country, but with many villages in it. The next day we got to Culm, once a famous place and a hanfe-town, but it has long been in decay, and is now, though a large place, filled with nothing but beggars

and

and ruins.   The fituation is upon a hill, and
would if the town was well built, be very pleafant.   From hence we paffed the 28th through
Thorn to Wladiflaw; the former of thefe
towns was a hanfe, and a noted place for
trade before that of Dantzick, but moft of its
commerce, and inhabitants are gone; it has
ftill, however, a good appearance, the ftreets are
broad, ftrait, and fome of them well paved,
and the houfes large and handfome: here is
yet fome trade by means of the Viftula, which
is what keeps the place from the ruin into
which fo many others have fallen. The country
we paffed is not fandy, but feems to be a good
loam, and the appearance of the corn in-
dictates good hufbandry, but many eftates
are quite defolate; we went through three
villages that had been reduced to afhes more
than a year ago, and no figns yet of being rebuilt.   Wladiflaw is a pretty well built town
alfo on the Viftula; the only buildings in it
that are of any note is the Cathedral; it being
the fee of a bifhop, an old Gothic edifice, and
the bifhop's palace, which has been much
damaged by a fiege the town ftood.

The 29th we went 30 miles to Plockfkow,
on the banks of the river, except where
marfhes prevent; the furrounding country is
a very rich foil, and not having fuffered from

an

an enemy, fhewed many figns of good cultivation: great champain tracks of open country are covered with wheat, which looked very
well: the ploughs were bufy in preparing
for barley—no oats are cultivated here. The
land feemed very well tilled by a couple of
little horfes and two oxen: but the ploughs
are of a moft aukward conftruction, and the
peafants know not how to turn a ftraight fur-
row; they go as crooked as can well be i-
magined, which is difagreeable to look at, tho'
I apprehend not the worfe for the corn. They
fow a good deal of hemp and flax in this
neighbourhood, which they are very well fituated for fending, with their corn to Dantzick. Wheat produces two quarters an acre;
barley three, and peafe two and an half. An
acre of hemp, or of flax is worth about fifty
fhillings. They have large herds of cattle,
which they feed in fummer in the marfhes
on the Viftula; and in winter upon cabbages
and turneps, which they always boil in the
German manner before they give them to the
cattle: this is not of much confequence
where wood is fo plentiful; but in England
would do only in the neighbourhood of coal
mines. But it is highly worthy of trial, to
fee how it would anfwer to follow this cuftom;
becaufe, if one acre boiled goes as far as three

or four raw, which I have heard it does, there
are many fituations in which it would be very
advifeable. We paffed near a nobleman's man-
fion, furrounded by a double moat—full of
water, and fome cannon mounted on the bat-
tlements; my fellow-traveller told me, that
this caftle had been often befieged by the op-
pofite party; but the nobleman driving all his
peafants and cattle immediately in, had yet
been fuccefsful in repelling them, which
feems to be the only fyftem of life in Poland
for any perfon to have the leaft fecurity; but
of late he has had the fortune to efcape any
ravages, and is remarkable for the induftry
and attention with which he cultivates his e-
ftate, and takes a moft fatherly care of all
the peafants on it.   This is a very rare inftance
in Poland; for they are generally ufed, as I have
often obferved, in a moft oppreffive manner;
but the good effect of this contrary treatment
is extremely vifible in the cafe of this nobleman, who, tho' with only a fmall eftate compared with many in the kingdom, has by
means of a regular and confiftent conduct towards his vaffals, and by a conftant attention
to the culture of his land been able to fave
much money, part of which he has laid out
in fortifying his caftle, which has more than
once preferved his property and his peafants,
                                                    and

and the reft is lodged in the bank of Dantzick.

The 30th we reached Zadrzin, which is a
ftage of more than forty miles, through a
very fine rich country, part of which is fully
cultivated : They fow very large quantities of
wheat and barley, but no rye, or oats, peafe
or beans; they fallow their lands for wheat,
and alfo lay all their dung in for it, and afterwards take two fucceffive crops of barley;
ploughing thrice for each. Wheat yields four
quarters an acre, and barley three. They
alfo fow fome hemp and flax, and get as fine
crops as any in Poland. The country is divided into four eftates, and has efcaped being
plundered, which is owing I fuppofe, to the
vicinity of the capital, where there has generally been a pretty ftrong garrifon. All this
country on the Viftula, and between Dantzick and Warfaw, is the beft fituated of any in
Poland ; for the voyage to the former city is
fhort, and there are many populous and confiderable towns, particularly Warfaw, which
take off large quantities of the products at a
good market, which is an advantage of the
moft valuable kind.

From Zadrzin is only forty miles to Warfaw, the road running all the way within fight
of the Viftula; in fome places fkirting marfh-

es,

es, but in others all through an arable country. This we travelled the 1ſt of May, arriving at that city in the afternoon. It is the ſeat of government, the capital of the kingdom, and the reſidence of the King; yet there is nothing ſtriking in it. The ſtreets are many of them crooked and ill paved, the buildings have little of elegance in them, tho ſome new ones, few in number make a tolerable ſhew; theſe are houſes belonging to the Poliſh nobles, who make Warſaw their winter reſidence. The royal palace is a noble edifice, being beyond compariſon the fineſt building in Poland. The apartments are very ſpacious, and ſome of them new fitted up and furniſhed in the Engliſh manner, being executed by London artiſts, brought from thence at the king's expence: The room they call the Hall of Victory, from formerly having been a hall, is converted into a ſaloon hung with tapiſtry from Bruſſels; the ceiling, panels, door-caſes, and window frames all neatly executed in white carving gilt: The rooms are very numerous, and all the offices for a court extremely convenient. And here let me obſerve, that notwithſtanding the preſent troubles which diſtract the kingdom, yet there is a magnificence and a brilliancy diſplayed around the King of Poland, which

ſuits

fuits very ill with the ftate of his mind, than
which by all accounts nothing can be more
unhappy. His majefty is certainly a man of
quick parts, and has a truly patriotick con-
cern for the miferies of his kingdom, which
he is utterly unable to prevent: the ftate in
which he lives is the regular court, which the
republick maintains for all its kings; and it
is fo much a piece of republican magnificence, that the King has not all the offices
in it in his own power. The court days do
not exhibit any great circle of Polifh lords—
the moft confiderable in the kingdom are not
only in oppofition to the crown, but even in
open arms againft it. But the officers who
are obliged to attend the nobles of the King's
party, foreign minifters, and Ruffian officers,
all together fill the room pretty well. There
is a Polifh regiment of guards, of a thoufand
men, difciplined in the Pruffian manner, raifed
by the prefent King, and he often reviews
them; the officers as well as private men are
Poles, but none of them nobles; they are
collected from all the other claffes, and depend abfolutely on the will of the King; this
is a meafure which was brought about by degrees, and with great art: it has been of uncommon confequence to the King; for by
means of this body of troops, he has been able

to

to move into several parts of the kingdom, without the guard of a Ruffian army, which is a moft unpopular, tho' a very neceffary mea-fure at prefent; on moft occafions it is not clear-ly known from what fund the King is able to pay this regiment, tho' his œconomy and private fortune would in better times eafily accomplifh it; but the publick revenue in the midft of the prefent confufions, fuffers extremely. If he is able to augment this corps by degrees, introducing none but men of low birth, mere foldiers of fortune, and abfolutely dependent on him; it may in time be a means of giving him an authority, which no other meafure will ever bring about, for Poland will never fee times of tolerable order, till her kings have abundantly more power than at prefent, and nothing but force will ever give them that power.

The fortifications of Warfaw, are fufficient to prevent the town being infulted by flying parties, or fmall armies, but could not ftand a fiege of any duration againft an army well provided; it has two good walls, flanked by many baftions and tolerably lined with ar-tillery; the ditch is broad and deep, and the waters of the Viftula may be let into it at pleafure. But the extent of thefe fortifica-tions is too great to be defended effectually
with

with lefs than eight thoufand men. Warfaw
is populous; being the capital of Poland, always brought great numbers to fettle in it,
which the miferable ftate of moft of the other
towns in the kingdom has lately increafed
very much, fo that the number of its inhabitants are computed to be above eighty thoufand.
There are at prefent in it many Polifh families, once in affluence, but now reduced to
live in a very mean way: I am told that feveral cities in the Queen of Hungary's, and
King of Pruffia's dominions are alfo full of
them; Dantzick and Koningfburg, I know
are. To what a fhocking ftate is this fine country reduced! wholly by the furious zeal
of Roman-catholick bifhops, who would never be fatisfied without the total deftruction
of the Proteftants and Greeks.

Upon our journey from Dantzick, we met
with a fmall party that attacked us, and
were more than once in fight of a band
of robbers, who would have deftroyed us, had
we been lefs guarded. This determined me
in the journey I propofed making to Breflaw,
to wait till I could go in fome company that
would be a protection. Fortunately this offered in a week, by the Dutch refident returning home by the route of Breflaw; he had a
party of Ruffian foldiers for his protection,

S 4   and

and I was informed that I fhould lay in
plenty of provifions and wine for our journey,
as we fhould pafs through a country that was
nine parts in ten deftroyed.   The 7th of May
we fet out, and reached Rava the 9th ; the
diftance about threefcore miles ; the firft five
from Warfaw under cultivation, but all the
reft one continued defart, and as pitiable a
fight as could well be feen.   This line of
country was not long fince well peopled, and
as well cultivated as any in Poland, which I
could fee by the numerous ruins of villages,
fingle cottages, and feats, fome quite deftroyed, others tumbling down, and many in
afhes : the country had moft of it been arable,
but the plough had no longer any bufinefs
here ; all the territory prefented one face of
defolation, the fields over-run with weeds,
and becoming grafs, without any cattle to
feed on them.   Rava was once a pretty town,
and well peopled ; but it is now a heap of
ruins : out of ten thoufand people that once
lived here, there does not remain above feventeen houfes inhabited, and thofe by fome
miferable creatures, too old to fly from the
misfortunes of their town.

From Rava to Sirad is one hundred miles ;
in which track of country, though it evidently
has all been cultivated, we faw but three vil-

3   lages

lages inhabited; all the reft burnt, and the
people gone: the inhabitants of thefe yet
venture to till a fmall quantity of land: we
faw a little wheat, and feveral ploughs turning in barley; but who will reap it, the
feedfmen little know. It is aftonifhing that
the country from Dantzick to Warfaw fhould
efcape fo well, while this has fuffered fo feverely. I there faw many devaftations; but
they are nothing, compared with the condition. of thefe territories. Sirad was in arms
both within and without the walls; we therefore made a detour to the left, and paffed it.
From thence to the boundary of Silefia is
about forty miles; all which is one continued
fcene of ruin. This is a journey of near
two hundred miles; and a more melancholy
one can fcarcely be travelled. Moderately
fpeaking, I do not believe there are five
thoufand fouls left in the whole country,
Sirad excepted, the ftate of which town we
were acquainted with: you may every
where trace the plough; fome fields wholly
ploughed, others half, others juft begun, but
all over-run with weeds and grafs; fome remains of corn on the ground that never was
reaped: houfes, barns, ftables, and all buildings, either burnt down, or falling for want
of

of repairs. Imagination cannot paint any
fcene more dreadful. Thofe landlords only
are tolerably off, who fled to Germany at the
beginning of the troubles, and live in expectation of peace, when they may return to their
eftates; the property of them is left, and will,
on a pacification, enable them to recover
themfelves. But others who, in their defence, or to fave their buildings from fire,
bought off their enemies, met their fate at
laft, and cannot return without the load of
debts; fo that new buildings and fettlements
will be impracticable to them. I was affured
that there are fome hundreds of eftates in the
kingdom at prefent without any owners ex-
ifting, fo many whole families having been
deftroyed.

Travels

Travels through Germany.

CHAPTER VIII.

*Silefia — Breſlaw — Journey to Berlin — The
Country—Agriculture—Deſcription of Ber-
lin—Preſent State of the King of Pruſſia's
Forces, Revenues, &c.—Saxony—Leipſick—
Dreſden—State of the Electorate.*

NOTHING could be more ſtriking,
than the different appearance of Silefia
from that of Poland. We entered it the
13th, and found the country full of villages,
half of which at leaſt were peopled with
Poles ; the land all cultivated, and much of it
extremely well ; the houſes and cottages in
good repair ; with all the appearances of eaſe
and happineſs ; which formed ſuch a contraſt
to the wretchedneſs we had ſo lately ſeen,
that the view had the effect of making Silefia
appear a paradiſe. Much of this muſt certainly be occaſioned by the great increaſe of
population from ſuch numbers of Poles, who
fly to eſcape the miſeries that every where
deſolate and lay waſte their own country.
The King of Pruſſia has officers appointed
along all his frontiers, to ſee that all theſe
poor people are received, and to provide cottages for them as faſt as poſſible. In this
work

work the King is at no expence; he only grants them permiffion to build cottages on any waftes or commons that are not abfolute property; and his edict directs, that every neighbourhood fhould give all due affiftance to the new fettlers, and find them employment in hufbandry or manufactures, after the rate of the country; and for the maintenance of fuch as do not find employment, he directs a tax to be laid on the diftrict; but this cannot be lafting, as they have portions of land affigned them fufficient for their maintenance when brought into culture. Upon the waftes belonging to the crown, thefe portions are confiderable enough to form, when cultivated, fmall farms, that hereafter will yield the crown a good rent. I faw many of thefe poor people, and it is hardly credible how much they feemed to enjoy themfelves, on efcaping the miferies of Poland, and finding fuch an humane protection in the territories of the neighbouring princes. I am informed that the Emprefs Queen receives them in the fame manner in Moravia, Auftria, and Hungary; many of them are in Tranfilvania. All the King of Pruffia's long line of frontier, from the bottom of Silefia to Livonia, is open to them; and great numbers take refuge in every part of it. I before gave an account of the

the multitudes, to whom the Emprefs of
Ruffia gave protection; if all this is confidered, it muft at once be apparent, that the kingdom of Poland muft be amazingly depopulated, fince it cannot be doubted but feveral
millions of people, probably not lefs than
three or four, are driven out of the country, or
killed. Such a depopulation will take feveral
ages to recover: and ftill this evil continues,
without any appearance of its coming to
an end; fo that what the event will be, except leaving that country a mere defart, is
very difficult to know.

We travelled thirty miles before we reached
Breflaw. All this line of country is rich either in corn, meadow, or wood; the arable
lands feemed very well cultivated; the wheat
looked well, and the quantity of land occupied with it is confiderable: they alfo cultivate rye: the barley was all coming up, and
feemed to promife good crops: they do not
fow any oats; but they cultivate many cabbages as winter food for their cattle, and they
reckon them much better, and to laft longer
than turneps: potatoes they plant in large
quantities for Breflaw, which city confumes
a great deal of all the products of the earth;
a vaft advantage to all the neighbouring
country: the fmall potatoes they fatten their
hogs

hogs with. The river Oder is navigable there, which is another great benefit to the country, always keeping the markets brisk, which of all other circumstances is the most certain means of introducing good husbandry. The ease and happiness of the peasants in this country is the more surprizing, as their taxes are very heavy, and carry as much into the King's coffers almost as into their own pockets. It can be attributed only to the regularity of his Prussian majesty's government; for that monarch looks so much into all his affairs, that there is no such thing in his dominions as irregular oppression : no minister, no officer dares to lay the hand of power on the defenceless poor ; the King is their protector, and they had better be heavily taxed by him, than pay less, but be open with it to those numerous and accidental oppressions common in all other arbitrary governments.

Breslaw is a very extensive and well-built city : it is most advantageously situated on the Oder, upon the banks of which are some very fine streets ; they are strait, well paved, and with many very well-built houses. There are several squares in it, and many public buildings, worthy the attention of a traveller ; among which are several churches, the Jesuits college, the town-house, the arsenal, the quay,

quay, &c. It is a bifhop's fee, but the cathedral has nothing remarkable in it: alfo the
feat of an univerfity, which has for fome time
been in a flourifhing fituation. It was pretty
ftrongly fortified in the laft war; has a good
wall, a double ditch, feveral baftions and
ravelins, and a ftrong citadel; but the works
are fo extenfive, that they require an army to
defend them. The King keeps a garrifon
here of ten thoufand men; they are drawn up
in the great fquare every day, and go through
their exercifes, being as well-difciplined regiments as any in the King's fervice. There
certainly refults from this ftrong garrifon, and
the others throughout Silefia, which are all
proportionably numerous, great fecurity; of
which the laft war was a very ftriking proof;
for, undoubtedly, the King owed his preferva-
tion to the excellent order all his fortreffes were
in, and the numerous garrifons they were furnifhed with: had the Auftrians met him unpre-
pared, they would have at leaft wrefted Silefia
from him, and perhaps have made fome impreffion upon his hereditary dominions. There
are many churches and convents in the city;
but I did not hear of any thing in them that
was particularly worthy of attention. There
is a great trade carried on here by means of

the Oder, and especially since the canal was
cut between that and the Elbe, which com-
municates with Hamburgh. The articles
in which this commerce is particularly carried on, are linen and flax, corn, timber,
plank, &c. all which are staple commodities
in Silesia, and produced in very great plenty.
Most of the staves which form so great an
export at Hamburgh, come from this duchy;
and the quantity of oak timber and plank,
which is exported from it, is very considerable.
Upon all these articles the King lays a duty
on the exportation; which is a piece of wrong
politics of so flagrant a nature, that would
make one think his abilities those of a warrior
alone. The trade of Breslaw has declined a
little since the troubles broke out in Poland;
for in times of tranquillity in that kingdom,
this province exports large quantities of goods
thither, particularly linens, of which the
Poles buy more than any other nation;
but since the commencement of the civil war,
they have been too much impoverished to be able
to purchase any quantity worth mentioning.

The manufacture of linen in Silesia is very
considerable: it employs many thousands of
people, enriches the whole duchy, and brings
in a very considerable revenue to the King.

Most

Moſt of the linens which are bleached at Haerlam in Holland, and afterwards are ſo well known under the name of *Dutch*, are made in Sileſia : formerly immenſe quantities were conſumed in England ; but ſince the great ſucceſs which has attended the fabricks of Ireland and Scotland, this impolitic importation is come to nothing, and thereby vaſt ſums ſaved to Great-Britain.——At this place I leſſened my expences of travelling conſiderably, by paying off all my attendants, except my old Swiſs, Martin, who has rode through the beſt part of Europe with me.

The 16th I left Breſlaw, taking a poſt-chaiſe to Steinau, on the Oder ; the diſtance thirty miles. This line of country is remarkably fine, fully cultivated, and in general well peopled. Landed property here is much divided ; here and there is found an old baron's eſtate of great extent, around an old caſtle with all the marks of antiquity and grandeur ; but in general the lands belong to perſons enriched by trade and manufactures, which has had one excellent effect, that of diffuſing much more liberty among the peaſants than they have in other parts. Upon theſe eſtates, the lands are let in farms, as in England, and the peaſants, not being vaſſals to tenants, are

T 2   hired

hired in the manner of our day-labourers, which is the fyftem of all others the moft beneficial. A common rent, in their farms, is from feven to eleven fhillings an acre: wheat yields two quarters an acre; barley three; buck-wheat four: the flax grounds are all inclofed by ditches, and they reckon an acre that yields three pounds a very good one. They keep all their cattle in winter in houfes, and feed them with boiled cabbages and ftraw. They lay moft of the manure they make upon their cabbage grounds, in the culture of which plant they feem to be very attentive. They make great ufe of mud from the Oder as a manure, and value it fo much, that they go feveral miles for it. They plough their land with oxen; the ftructure of their ploughs is remarkable; they feem, from the height of the wheels, to be very well in-ftructed in the doctrine of the lever.

The 17th I reached Grumberg, through forty-five miles of very indifferent road; dining at Glogau, a pretty town, agreeably fituated on the Oder, very ftrongly fortified, and always garrifoned with two thoufand men. It was anciently the refidence of the dukes of Glogau, and there are remains of their palace in the caftle. The cathedral is a very ancient

4   and

and a fine building. They have fome linen
fabricks, and a good trade on the Oder. The
country around it, and quite to Grumberg,
is various, confifting of woods, arable, meadow, fome wafte, and alfo fome marfh land.
The villages are not very thick, and the peafants do not feem to be fo well off as thofe
nearer to Breflaw; what the reafon is, I
could not difcover.

My next day's journey was thirty miles,
through Croffen, to Frankfort on the Oder.
Croffen is the capital of a territory of the
fame name: it is a very well-built town,
having been rebuilt after a great fire which
happened at the beginning of this century:
the ftreets are ftrait, broad, and well paved:
it is adorned with an handfome town-houfe,
and five churches, one of which makes a good
figure, being fituated in the middle of a
fquare.

Frankfort is in Brandenburg, and was once
one of the moft confiderable cities in the
Empire, being an hanfe town, and an Imperial city; but it has loft moft of its privileges. It is divided into the old and new
town by the Oder, over which there is a
handfome bridge, inftead of an old wooden
one which was burnt in the laft war. The

T 3   ftreets

ſtreets are handſome, and many of the houſes
make a good figure, eſpecially thoſe which
have been built ſince the laſt war.   Their
trade is conſiderable, both with Berlin, Hamburgh, the Baltic, and all Sileſia; and before
the war raged in Poland, with that kingdom
alſo; ſo that it is one of the richeſt places in
the King's dominions.   They have an univer-
ſity, but it is not very well ſtocked with ſtu-
dents of any conſequence, though they have
two well-built colleges.   The town-houſe is
an handſome building; and the arſenal is
large and well filled.   The moſt agreeable
part of the town is the great market-place,
which is ſurrounded by the beſt houſes in the
place.

The ſoil around Frankfort is ſandy, and
not very well inhabited : there is much waſte
land, which might be cultivated to good profit, conſidering the near neighbourhood of ſo
many navigations, but encouragement ſeems
to be wanting.   I made many enquiries concerning the depredations of the Ruſſians here;
and from the information I could get, I have
reaſon to believe that the accounts we had in
England were much exaggerated : they burnt
ſome villages, and raiſed heavy contributions;
but as to utterly deſtroying a whole track of
country,

country, it was not true. Another circumftance I fhould remark, which is, the mifchief being all repaired which they did; for
I have yet feen no figns of any of that ruin
which fell from their hands : this is to be attributed to the good conduct of the King of
Pruffia, who, notwithftanding the general feverity of his government, very wifely favoured thofe parts of his dominions that fuffered
moft by war, as foon as the peace was
made.

The 18th carried me 36 miles to Berlin,
through a continued track of fand, yet tolerably cultivated in fome parts, but much of it a
dreary wafte, and very thinly peopled. They
find that the only very profitable crop upon
thefe fands is buck-wheat, which they fow in
large quantities, and they get a product which
equals the beft foils applied to that grain :
when a piece of land has been more carefully
managed than ordinary, it will yield a good
crop of rye; but as to wheat or barley, it is
hardly to be feen.

As I defigned to make fome ftay at Berlin,
I hired private lodgings; of which I had as
good for fifteen fhillings a week, as would
have coft me five and thirty at London. But
this city is not peopled proportionably to its

T 4   fize;

fize ; hence the general remark, that grafs is
feen in the ftreets, which is, however, only in
one neglected quarter of the town ; the other
parts are very well built ; the ftreets are remarkably fpacious, long, and well paved ; and
the buildings in general are fuch as certainly
rank it among the fineft cities in Europe.
Of the public edifices, thofe which are ufually
vifited by travellers are, the royal palace—the
arfenal—the churches of Notre Dame, St.
Nicholas, St. Martin, and the Romifh chapel
—the theatre—the equeftrian ftatue of Frederick the firft, &c. The palace is a magnificent but an unequal building, like all thofe
that are raifed at different times : fome of the
apartments are large, and well proportioned ;
but they by no means anfwered my expectations, either in dimenfions, fitting up, or furniture. The immenfity of filver remarked by
Mr. Hanway, when he was here, was all
melted in the late war, and very little of it is
reftored. Much of the furniture, for a royal
palace, is very mean ; but this we are not to
be furprized at, as the King gives his attention
to fo much greater objects. Some of the pictures are fine. The front of the arfenal would
be very beautiful, but, as the above-mentioned traveller juftly obferves, it is profufely
loaded

loaded with ornaments. I viewed the con-
tents, and was much entertained with them;
for, very contrary to what is feen in moft
other buildings under this name, here are no
ufelefs arms, nothing but what is ready for
immediate fervice. The train is a very fine
one. The theatre is in a moft grand ftile,
admirably contrived to give much magnificence to the reprefentation of operas. A very
few circumftances excepted, it deferves to be
confidered as a model for thefe buildings.
The Romifh chapel is a monfter of difpropor-
tion, but the portico is elegant. The equeftrian ftatue of Frederick the Firft is a fine
performance; the horfe is remarkably fine,
and there is much fpirit in the attitude of the
figure.

The fortifications of Berlin are regular; but
the city is of too great extent to have any
thing of ftrength, if attacked by a powerful
army. The number of inhabitants are reckoned at about an hundred thoufand. There
is always a garrifon of from eight to twelve
thoufand men in it. Charlottenburgh is a
fmall palace within a mile of Berlin; the
rooms of which are fmall, but very elegant:
it contains nothing that appears very ftriking
to a traveller; the ball-room is handfome,
but

but much exceeded by many others. The
gardens here, as well as at Potſdam, have
nothing in them but regularity, which is diſ-
guſting.   Sans Souci is a detached apartment
in a garden ; but nothing of this ſort that I
have ſeen abroad, is comparable to a number of
places we have in England : nor do I think
any of theſe palaces and boxes in the neighbourhood of Berlin are tolerable in taſte : the
only natural beauty they had was the river,
and that is moulded into a canal for them :
they have no verdure; the walks are ſand,
and the ſituations in general flats.

There is a good deal of commerce carried
on at Berlin, by means of the canals which
join the Spree and the Oder, and the Oder
and the Elbe ; by which means there is a moſt
advantageous communication with Hamburgh,
the Baltick, and all Sileſia.   This is of great
conſequence to the manufactures of Berlin,
which are numerous and flouriſhing : they
have fabricks of ſilk, ſtuffs, woollen cloths of
ſeveral ſorts, and in particular one which
clothes moſt of the army ; tapeſtry, laces,
glaſs, a little hardware, &c.   The King gives
great encouragement to all manufactures,
which has had a great effect in a place where
he found many fabricks fixed by French
refugees

refugees after the revocation of the edict of Nantes, whose posterity now carry on the principal trade of the city. Berlin supplies Silesia with great quantities of these goods; and before the civil war raged in Poland, that kingdom took off much. They have a small export to the Baltic; formerly to Sweden, but that is now no more.

I was twice or thrice at court, more to see the King, than for any other entertainment. I saw him about nine years ago, and was much surprized to find him so little altered. The immensity of fatigue, both of body and mind, which he went through during the last war, one would have apprehended must have entirely broke him; but he has, by a regular way of life, and great abstemiousness, both then and since, prevented any ill effects. Bodily fatigue may be physick, and mental labour not very destructive, but anxiety is the destroyer, against which it is very difficult to guard: for several years the King was uncertain of his fate; victories had little effect, defeats were ruinous, and he could scarcely conjecture whether he was to be stripped of several provinces, or even his whole dominions. In such a situation, we may easily conceive that anxiety must commit great ravages on

him;

him; and I muft own myfelf furprized to fee
his health continue fo good. His principal
amufement is exercifing his troops; to fee
them, is one of the moft entertaining fights
at Berlin. It is thought that the King himfelf has not fo nice an eye as formerly to the
minutiæ of the tactic, but his officers keep
it up in the higheft perfection. His army is
at prefent more numerous, and better provided than ever ; they do not fall fhort of
one hundred and forty thoufand men; and
there is not a regiment in his fervice that is
not ready for marching : his whole army, artillery, baggage, and all attendants, could be
in the field upon a week's notice at any time ;
his fortreffes are all in better order than before
the laft war, and fome places made of great
ftrength upon the frontiers of Silefia, which
never before were fortified at all. His trea-
fure is reported to be confiderable, and he
certainly is not encumbered with debts ; for
the laft war, immenfe as it was to him, did
not make him contract a fhilling of debt, tho'
it is certain his antagonift, the Queen of
Hungary, anticipated many of her revenues.
If all things are confidered, it will appear
very evident, that his power is better eftablifhed than ever, and that he has no profpect
of

of feeing another confederacy, which will bear
fo hard upon him as the laft. Auftria will not
be eager to attack him, after having failed, with
every poffible advantage on her fide. If fhe
could not wreft Silefia from him, when
France, Ruffia, Sweden, and Saxony were in
alliance with her, and their power fo actually
brought to bear upon him, that he fought bat-
tles with them all; fuch a confederacy is
not to be looked for in an age; and if it failed
in its aim, that aim may be pronounced impracticable. Saxony, it cannot be expected
will unite again, unlefs it be with Pruffia, but
the fituation of it confidered, if it proves an
enemy, it will be an enemy fwallowed up as
in the laft war, and the country made to contribute amply to pay the expence of it.
Ruffia will fcarcely unite againft the King,
with whom fhe is now in clofe alliance; it
would be extremely contrary to her intereft.
France will always be found in full employment by England; fhe will not quickly fend
armies againft Pruffia. The King therefore
has the fatisfaction of enjoying peace.

Thefe are the ideas of the Berlin politicians, who all declare the peace will be lafting, from the great jealoufy of Auftria, and
Ruffia, either oppofing or uniting with each
other :

other: every party is ſtrongly armed, and looks on in ſilence, except Ruſſia, who, knowing her own ſtrength and fearleſs of conſequences, carries on a moſt extenſive war with Turkey and in Poland.

The King's revenues amount at preſent, to about a million and an half ſterling; a ſum which in England appears ſmall; but if the different value of money there, and in Brandenburg be conſidered; and likewiſe, the uncommon exertions of œconomy unequalled in any other court; this ſum, I am confident, is in the King's hands as good as four millions, perhaps as five in England. The land-tax throughout his dominions is regular, and equals about nine ſhillings in the pound: the crown lands yield a conſiderable rent, and are as well managed to profit, as a private gentleman's eſtate. The cuſtoms are but a ſmall article; they are gathered in his ports on the Baltick and at Embden. The exciſe is general on all the neceſſaries of life, and riſes ſo high as forty per cent. Theſe taxes are very heavy; but ſuch is the regularity of his government, and ſo little oppreſſion is met with from miniſters and revenue-officers, that the people are beyond compariſon happier than in the dominions of Saxony, Auſtria, ftria, or Bavaria. Much of his fuccefs in the late war, was doubtlefs owing to the fubfidy he received from England: the difcontinuance of which, and the breaking off all connections between the two courts, ftruck hard upon him; for it took him out of the hands of France, from whom he received a fubfidy of three hundred thoufand pounds a year, and left him without an equivalent from England. The treatment he received from the latter country, upon the change of that miniftry which had conducted the war, made an impreffion upon him much againft England, of whom he has often expreffed himfelf with fome acrimony: what the refult will be in future political arrangements, is not eafy to fay; but if the connection continues between France and Auftria, that between England and Pruffia, muft in the nature of things be renewed; for when one part of Europe throws itfelf into an alliance offenfive to the reft— a counter alliance muft ever be formed, or all good ideas of politicks be abfolutely given up.

The 1ft of June I left Berlin, and got to Britzen, the diftance thirty miles: all which track of country is very fandy, though tolerably populous, and fome of it well cultivated.

tivated. They fow much buck-wheat; and were now ploughing for turneps, which they fow the middle of this month : and I believe this root and buck-wheat, with a very little rye, to be all the products thefe poor fands yield, and yet they feem to be very well manured; for the countrymen houfe their cattle in winter, and raife by that means large quantities of dung, which they mix with a kind of ftiff earth, which they dig from under the fand; a compoft which I fhould fuppofe, muft agree extremely well with fuch dry barren foils.

The 2d I advanced no further than Wittenburg, the diftance only 15 miles. In this journey I paffed from Brandenburg to Saxony, and the foil changes almoft immediately for the better, and the population of the country alfo. The foil is a good loam, which yields tolerable crops of wheat; they have alfo barley, and I remarked a few pieces of flax. Wittenburg was noted before the laft war for its cloth manufactories, and for dying better than at any other place in the electorate; the latter bufinefs is yet found here, though not near fo much as formerly; but moft of its fabricks are removed to Berlin, fo that the place

place has not been able to recover the ruin it met with in the war.   Martin Luther's church is yet ftanding, tho' three hundred years old, and has feen fo many fieges, cannonades, and bombardments without any damage.

The 3d I went to Leipfick, the diftance 30 miles, through a country naturally exceedingly fertile, but carries many marks of the miferies of the late war.   Moft of it has been well cultivated, but upon riding into feveral fields now in grafs, and whofe appearance indicates wretched management,   I found they had been arable ones within a few years ; and upon making enquiries,   I had feveral fpots pointed out to me,   whereon ftood fmall villages,   confifting of farm-houfes, now no more ; and all the lands which belonged to them, and once yielded abundant crops of corn, are now little better than wafte and common foreft land,   whereon the tenants of the fame landlord turn their cattle.   This is not the cafe with two or three places, but continues for many miles ; and is owing to the nobles to whom the country belongs, having ruined themfelves with paying military contributions fo often, that at laft, they had nothing to pay when their buildings were burnt down,   and themfelves left too poor to erect new ones: This is generally the reafon, why the feat of war is fo very injurious to a country; for nothing is fo great an evil, as land cultivated, formerly belonging to owners, too poor to raife the buildings ne-ceffary for bringing it again into culture.   If the landlords of fuch a country would allow every thing to be deftroyed the firft campaign, they would be reduced it is true; but then they would be free from thofe enormous debts which not only carry their ruin with them to the graves of fuch as groan under them, but entail mifery upon their children.

Leipfick, the fuburbs included, is one of the moft confiderable cities in this part of Germany, notwithftanding its having fuffer-ed very feverely in the two laft wars, and felt fome heavy ftrokes, which are not yet recovered.   It has been the theatre of almoft every war that has happened in Germany. In the famous one of thirty years, it was very often taken and retaken by the Swedes, and Imperialifts; no lefs than five times in two years: It felt the weight of Charles XII's invafion of Saxony, than whom there have been few more brutal invaders.   And the two laft wars fucceeded each other very quick-ly; its trade and buildings much declined in them.

them. The city itfelf is not an agreeable place, from the narrownefs of the ftreets, and the height of the houfes, which rife to eight or nine ftories; but the fuburbs are much more fpacious and better built; they are alfo pleafant, from the number of areas, and gardens in them; and from the conflux of three fmall rivers. They have not many publick buildings at Leipfick that much deferve a ftranger's attention; the beft among them is St. Nicholas Church, which is a very fine edifice. The town-houfe is an old but a good ftructure; the exchange is another: and around the great market place are many houfes of private merchants, which make an uncommon figure for buildings of that fort; but there are feveral traders in the city, that have made confiderable fortunes, and before the laft war treble the number; but the greateft among them upon the breaking out of it, removed themfelves and their effects to Hamburgh. The univerfity is one of the moft famous in Germany, and much frequented by ftudents of family and fortune; but this alfo declined much in the laft war.

Trade is the foul of Leipfick: Confidering that it is an inland place, and without the advantage even of a navigable river, the great-

nefs

nefs of its commerce is very furprizing ; but
it is owing to its fairs, of which they have
three very confiderable ones every year. To
them merchants bring or fend goods of all
forts from every part of Europe : all the manufactures of Germany, France, Italy, England, Holland, and Flanders are met with
here : Vaft magazines are formed of Eaft India goods of all forts ; of Weft India commodities ; of wines, brandies, fruits, filk,
hemp, flax, iron, and in a word all forts of
products : And purchafers refort hither from
every part of Germany and the North.
Thefe fairs alfo carry off great quantities of
the fabricks which are made at Leipfick, of
which there are feveral forts ; fuch as filk,
cotton and woollen manufactures, paper,
gold, and filver laces, &c. but all thefe fuffered much from the laft war ; nor have
they recovered themfelves to any thing like
their former fuccefs : Indeed, I obferved in
converfation with feveral merchants here,
that they had all a diftruft that they were by
no means fecure from frefh vifits of the Pruffians ; and while this is the cafe, (at which
we cannot be furprized) it is not to be wondered that commerce and manufactures do
not thrive.   The injury the whole Electorate
                                    fuftained

fuftained laft war, in the deftruction of its manufactures and trade; the ruin of its agriculture, and the decline of its population, was of an exceedingly great amount, and fuch as cannot be recovered without the moft unremitting attention, and political conduct of half a century; before which time it will probably fee in fome caufe or other, a renewal of its calamities. If thefe circumftances are confidered, with the oppreffive government of all the German princes that have an abfolute authority, we fhall have reafon to wonder at any trade at all being found in Saxony.

The 6th, I travelled thirty miles to Meiffen, through the fineft part of Saxony; and which, notwithftanding the fury of the late war, is now a populous and a well cultivated country; there is a great deal of arable land, and very fine champain fields, covered with corn; many villages, and the people feemed to be active, and quite alive in their bufinefs. Part of the females were collected in fmall knots in the villages fpinning wool; others drove the horfes and oxen that drew the ploughs; this employment of the women is an excellent fign, where the men do not, in confequence, indulge in idlenefs, which is the cafe in fome countries. They cultivate a great deal of wheat and barley, and were now fowing fome

U 3   buck-

buck-wheat; but it is a grain for which
their lands are too good, the pooreſt ſands
will rival them: They cultivate turneps, cabbages; and alſo cabbages for feeding themſelves and their cattle; their herds are numerous; they feed them not only in their meadows, but alſo upon clover, of which I ſaw
ſeveral large pieces, a thing I had not remarked of a long time. I enquired into their
management of it; they ſow it with barley,
and in the ſucceeding year, either mow it
twice for hay, thrice ſometimes; or elſe feed
ſheep, young cattle, cows, oxen, and horſes
upon it: the hay they prefer to meadow hay.
They keep it two years upon the ground, and
after that plough it up for any ſort of crop,
but do not ſeem to conſider it as a peculiar
preparation for wheat, which is the idea in
England: It has not been long cultivated
here, but ſpreads very faſt, from their finding the profit of it to be great. The lands
here are cultivated by both the landlords and
peaſants; the latter are in general farmers,
and not of very little ſpots, but they are
bound to apply a part of their time with their
teams, &c. to cultivate thoſe parts of the
eſtate, which the landlord holds in his own
hands, and which are uſually pretty conſiderable.

                                        Meiſſen

Meiffen is a little town, weakly fortified,
but with a ftrong caftle on the Elbe; it is
only remarkable (the Drefden Porcelane excepted) for a covered bridge of wood over
that river; the cathedral I had been told was
a fine building, with many fine electoral mo-
numents in it, but I found it worthy of very
little obfervation.   The manufacture of Porcelane, was once more famous here, than at
any other place in Europe, but the laft war
almoft ruined it; upon the King of Pruffia's
irruption into Saxony, moft of the workmen,
and the materials were removed; but the war
continuing fo long, and Saxony remaining
in the hands of the Pruffians, fome of the
people died, and others were loft; fome the
King of Pruffia fecured, and fent them to
Berlin; where he attempted to eftablifh a
fimilar manufactory, but he has executed nothing comparable to the old Drefden pieces.
Upon the eftablifhment of peace, the works
at Meiffen were reftored,   and a frefh fet
of workmen, with fome old ones, refumed
the manufactory: I have feen the beft pieces
they have made, and fhall venture to affert,
that the manufacture is loft; for they are not
in the clearnefs of the white, to be compared
with the metal formerly made; as to fine
painting, it is any where to be had, and there-

U 4   fore

fore not peculiar to the Drefden ware. This is a great lofs to the curious, and lovers of fine Porcelane all over Europe ; and the more fo, as none of the numerous fabricks fet up in England, France, or Holland, have come near equal to it.

The 17th I reached Drefden, which is only fifteen miles from Meiffen, through the moft beautiful line of country I have feen in Germany; it is all hill and dale, corn, vines, and meadows along the banks of the Elbe a continued picture; the river is every where feen to advantage, with the beautiful circumftance of the banks being high and woody; a more entertaining picturefque fcene can hardly be viewed.

Drefden I can eafily conceive, was before the deftruction of the fuburbs, one of the fineft cities in Europe ; but the Pruffians have much reduced its beauty, by burning down a great part of the moft beautiful quarters of it. The old city is fortified in a regular manner ; the baftions are of ftone ; and there is a double ditch, but yet the ftrength of it is nothing, unlefs the garrifon be very numerous : The river Elbe divides it into two cities, the old and the new. The bridge over that river which is built of ftone, is reckoned the fineft in Germany ; but no perfon who has

feen

feen that at Weftminfter, will think there
is either beauty or magnificence in it.   It is
five hundred and forty feet long, thirty fix
broad, and confifts of nineteen arches.   The
electoral palace is not a very ftriking building
for the beauties of architecture ; but there are
many very fine and fpacious apartments in it
very fplendidly furnifhed ; much of it done
fince the war ; for fome of the beft furniture
was ruined by the Pruffians, and a vaft number of curiofities carried off.   The King it is
fuppofed, did not defign to touch any thing,
and no commander keeps a more regular difcipline, but in fo long a war fo full of events,
and thofe remarkably fevere ; a place of curiofities, muft neceffarily fare but badly.   The
ftables form a magnificent building, being
very fpacious, and were once filled with fome
of the fineft horfes in Germany, but many of
the ftalls are now unoccupied ; indeed the
revenues of the electorate fuffered to fo great
a degree in the late war, that Drefden has
ever fince exhibited a very different appearance ; the court is no longer what it was,
and all thofe circumftances which flow from
great revenues, have funk proportionably to
the decline, which the Saxon income has experienced.   No court in Germany was fo profufe ; but there is an œconomy in it now,

which

which promiſes a much happier adminiſtra-
tion of affairs than has been experienced in
the two laſt.

The Romiſh chappel is one of the fineſt
edifices at Dreſden; it is a well-proportioned
and magnificent building; moſt highly orna-
mented: It was built for the private uſe of
the late King and his court.

The chamber of curioſities, have yet a great
many very beautiful models, and toys, which
cannot fail entertaining any traveller; and
the collection which they call the Kunts-kam-
mar, which is chiefly of natural rarities, equal
to any thing that can be ſeen; but as the particulars of theſe things have been publiſhed
by more than one traveller, I ſhall not ſwell
theſe pages with a recital of them. The
gallery of pictures, is equal to moſt that are to
be ſeen in Italy; and are kept in admirable
preſervation. The pieces by Correggio are
to be equalled no where but in Parma. A
very magnificent work, containing plates of
all the pictures in this gallery, was publiſhed
at Dreſden, under the direct inſpection of the
late King.

The Indian palace, of which ſeveral writers have given long accounts, is in my opinion a very ſilly affair; and by no means even
elegant. Count Bruhl's famous palace ſuffered

fered moſt ſeverely in the war, at which nobody was concerned, from the foundation of
all his grandeur being laid in the miſeries of
the Saxons; and from his being the principal
plotter, and adviſer of that war, which ruined his maſter.   The picture gallery is
one of the fineſt rooms I have any where
ſeen.

From the beſt accounts I could get while
at Dreſden, the decline in all the affairs of
conſequence throughout the government of
Saxony, upon account of the late war, is
much greater than has been thought by ſome
authors who have written lately.   Before the
war, the revenues of the electorate, by means
however of very great oppreſſion, amounted
to a million and an half ſterling; but I was aſ-
ſured, that they do not at this day, although
near ſeven years of peace have intervened, riſe
to ſeven hundred thouſand pounds, and yet
the government is burthened with a very heavy
debt.   Saxony, before the war, contained
near two millions of people; it has not now
much above one: In Dreſden were an hundred and ten thouſand people, but at preſent
it would be difficult to find half the number;
ſuch ſtrong marks of decline are not to be
miſtaken, they ſhew the ſeverity of the late
war, in the moſt ſtriking colours; and prove

clearly

clearly that if it had continued much longer, the whole electorate would have been made a defart.

The prefent government conducts all things in a very fenfible and political manner; they find the wretched ftate of the country will admit of nothing but an œconomy which has not been practifed in this country for a long while; the people fee and know the publick diftrefs, and do not repine at the taxes they are forced to pay, as all did when the amount was fquandered by count Bruhl, and the King, in cloaths, toys, and gewgaws. Only fifteen thoufand regular troops are kept up, but they have five or fix thoufand militia regularly difciplined. This is certainly acting with prudence; for the whole country is fo impoverifhed, that if they raifed by taxes a revenue to do otherwife, it muft be by the ruin of the people. They muft have time not only to recruit their loffes, but alfo their numbers. The foil is in general fertile, and the Saxons are induftrious enough to bring it into culture, if they have time given them, without making even peace itfelf too burthenfome, by taxation, and without hurrying them into another war, which could not fail of being ruinous to the whole electorate. Some encouragement has been given to agriculture and

and manufactures fince the peace; particularly by an exemption from taxes in certain cafes wherein they would be extremely burthenfome; but the effential foundation of tolerable cultivation, or activity in carrying on fabricks, is wanting, which is wealth, or at leaft eafy circumftances in the undertakers; but this electorate, the Pruffians exhaufted to fo great a degree, that they left fcarcely any wealth in it; the lands are in the hands of nobility fo reduced, that they can fcarcely live; much lefs are able to carry on improvements in the manner requifite at prefent, for being effectual in reviving hufbandry in their country; and when this is the cafe, fuch a renovation muft be left to common caufes, the increafe of the people, and of induftry among the lower claffes, which is always of moft flow operation.

The amazing difference of the event of the war to Brandenburg and Saxony, is ftriking. The latter is fo ruined and exhaufted, as to lye almoft at the mercy of any invader; without people, trade, revenues, or forces, on a comparifon with what all thofe articles were before the war: on the contrary, the King of Pruffia is in poffeffion of as great an income as ever; a finer army, than when he began the war: his dominions fuffered indeed, but the

3   wounds

wounds feem to have been but fkin-deep:
certainly his country was not made the feat
of war in the manner he made that of the
Elector of Saxony. The contraft indeed is
fo ftriking, that if ever a new war breaks out
between Pruffia and Auftria, Saxony moft undoubtedly will not join the latter.

The 12th I fet out from Drefden, and got
to Lentmeritz, in Bohemia, in two days,
paffing through Pirna, and by the famous
caftle of Koningftein. Pirna is a little place
among the mountains, and Koningftein is a
caftle fituated on the top of a rock, three
hundred feet high, and half a mile in circumference. The way to it is fo difficult, that a
company is fufficient to defend it againft an
army. In it is a well, above fixteen hundred
feet deep, which fupplies the garrifon with
water. In the labyrinth of thefe rocks and
mountains, the King of Pruffia caught the
Saxon army and made them prifoners. The
country is in general very wild and romantic,
and the views of the Elbe running through
fuch a region of mountains extremely gro-
tefque : There are fome vineyards planted upon
fouthern fpots of thefe mountains, where the
grapes ripen tolerably, but the wine is not
drinkable to thofe who have been ufed to that
which is good.

CHAP-

CHAPTER IX.

Journey acrofs Bohemia—Prague—Defcription of the country—The people—Nobility—Hufbandry--Manufactures--Moravia--Olmutz--Brinn—Journey to Vienna—Defcription of the capital.

LENTMERITZ is a fmall town in Bohemia, fituated on the river Elbe; it has fome fortifications, but none of any great ftrength : near this place the King of Pruffia gained a great victory over the Auftrians in the laft war. The neighbouring country was feveral times the feat of war, and fuffered much : part of the mifchiefs done, are not yet recovered ; for there are feveral tracks of land belonging to a Bohemian nobleman, who refides at Vienna, which were once arable, but are now over-run with grafs and weeds, and ftill have by no means near a ftock of cattle proper for the land ; and fome villages are of a very poor appearance with feveral houfes almoft burnt down, that have not yet been repaired. The country that is cultivated, does not feem to be managed in an able manner ;

ner ; and the peasants are much worse treated
than they are in Saxony.

The 18th I reached Prague, the capital of
Bohemia, and one of the largest cities in Europe. The country through which the road
runs is various; much of it is of a fruitful soil,
and tolerably cultivated in some parts, but
there are in every track many marks of bad
husbandry and inattention, greatly owing I
suppose to a want of industry, and partly to the
oppression which the peasants experience:
They have some tolerable crops of wheat,
but I never saw worse barley, or any corn
more full of weeds; and they value it so
little, that on various pieces of barley and
pease I saw cattle feeding, which made me
enquire if they were sown with intention to
be eat green ; but that was not the case ; it
is a mere instance of stupid neglect. I observed one or two pieces of flax, which looked
very well. The winter food of their cattle is
principally the cabbage, turnep, and red cabbage, which they cultivate in large quantities. I saw several young plantations of them,
but they do not seem to manage them well.

Prague is very well situated on the river
Muldaw ; it is divided into two cities by that
river. The fortifications are regular, and
much

much fuperior to what they were before the
laft war ; but the city is of fo great an extant,
that it requires an army to defend it. It fuffered very much by the fiege it ftood in the
beginning of the war againft the King of Pruffia, who cannonaded and bombarded it in fo
fevere a manner, that not many buildings
efcaped; whole quarters were beat down, or
burnt, and I was fhewn feveral very large
gardens and young orchards, which before
that fiege were entirely covered with houfes,
then deftroyed, and the people are too poor to
rebuild them in a place where there are yet
more houfes than are occupied : fcarcely any
of the publick buildings efcaped damage at
the fame fiege. The univerfity is one of the
moft famous in Germany, and has a vaft
number of ftudents; the people at Prague
talk of five thoufand ; what they might be
formerly I know not, but at prefent they are
fhort of three thoufand. In 1409, when John
Hufs was rector, it is a fact that there were
thirty thoufand ftudents here. The Jefuits
college is one of the fineft buildings in the
city, but it fuffered by feveral unlucky cannon balls, and is not yet thoroughly repaired.
The bridge, which joins the old and the new
town, is fifteen hundred and eighty feet long,
by thirty broad, and has feventeen arches, and

is all of ftone; it is a folid edifice, has nothing of elegance in it; and when a traveller
hears that it was an hundred and fifty years a
building, he will fuppofe it muft have been in
an age extremely poor, or been undertaken
by a prince of little fpirit. The fineft edifices
in the world are rarely thofe which were fo
long in raifing. St. Peter's at Rome is an inftance againft me, but St. Paul's at London,
and the bridge at Weftminfter, are ftrong
ones in my favour, and many more might be
quoted. The royal palace, and the cathedral,
are very mean buildings that contain fcarcely
any thing worthy of notice. What at Prague
are much the beft worth feeing, are the palaces of the nobility; fome of which are very
noble edifices, that would make a great figure
in the beft built cities of Italy; feveral of
them are of very great fize, with moft fpacious
apartments, and very magnificent furniture.
Thofe of the princes Lobcowitz, and Ifchar-
nan, and the counts Galas, Straka, Czaflaw,
and Manftein, deferve particular attention;
they contain many apartments that are worthy
of fovereign princes, but the number of very
good pictures is trifling.

Moft of the Bohemian nobility, who are a
numerous body, keep their refidence in winter at Prague, and in fummer on their eftates.

None

None of them refort to Vienna, but fuch as
are in office in the court, which is a very uncommon inftance.   It is their prefence in this
city that alone fupports it; for without their
refort, and the garrifon, which is generally
pretty numerous, the city would be a defart;
being utterly deftitute of both trade and manufactures: the univerfity does fomething,
but not much.   All the lower claffes here are
poor; the burghers are treated by the nobles
very contemptuoufly, to a degree not common elfewhere; if the place was ever fo well
fituated for trade, or manufacture, this would
be a fure means of damping their progrefs.

The 16th I left Prague, and went to Nym-
burg, a fmall town twenty five miles diftant;
the country various, but much of it pretty
tolerably cultivated; rather better than the
track to the north of Prague.   The peafants
are treated in a wretched manner; they have
hovels of the worft fort to live in, little better
than thofe in Weftphalia; being loofe ftones
laid on one another for the walls, and the cre-
vices filled with mud, and the covering fome
ftrong poles, with turf fpread on them, and
a hole at top in the middle is all the chimney
that any of them have; adjoining is their
barn, built of the fame materials, in which
they ftow their little corn, and keep their

X 2   cattle

cattle in winter; each cottage has a few acres of land around it, with a cow or two, and a miferable pair either of horfes, or oxen for ploughing their land. In general, Sunday is the only day in the week which they are allowed for cultivating this land, in order to raife provifions for fubfifting on the whole week; but in feed-time and harveft, their lords indulge them with another: When I fpeak therefore of the hufbandry of the country, I do not mean of the peafants, nor of the farmers, for there is fcarcely any fuch thing, but of the nobility, and other landlords, who all cultivate their own eftates by means of their agents and ftewards. The peafants in every refpect refemble nearly thofe of Poland, than whom they are not favoured more.

At firft fight it may appear, that landlords, who act upon this fyftem, muft make far more of their eftates, than thofe who let them, in the Englifh manner, to farmers, becaufe here the profit of the farmer is confolidated with that of the landlord; but, from the repeated obfervations which I have often had occafion of making, I am convinced that the cafe is the very contrary. If any eftate was only of fuch a fize as to form a good farm, it would be very true; but eftates are thus cultivated

tivated whofe extent is from twenty to thirty thoufand acres of cultivated land, either meadow, pafture, arable, fheep-walk, or woods, all in fome culture or other, and a vaft track arable. To be forced to cultivate fuch immenfe farms, they are obliged to have fwarms of bailiffs and agents. In every place where a farm-houfe fhould be, is a bailiff's houfe, who manages a certain track of land. Thus the landlord is at the monftrous expence of ftocking his whole eftate, and running all the chances of that ftock, and at the fame time has to keep as many bailiffs as if they were farmers, and who all live out of the land before he has his clear profit, as much as if they were farmers; with this great diftinction, that being merely fervants, they have little intereft in the fuccefs of their hufbandry, and confequently the mafter fuffers all the ufual inconveniences of fuch a fituation: his agents of all forts coft him as much as farmers would make for themfelves, fuppofing them honeft; and if they turn out otherwife, a great deal more. Thus he gets none of the farmers profit, at the fame time that he lofes the intereft of all the money employed in ftocking, and the chances to which that ftock is liable. From which ftate of the affair, I think it is very evident, how

X 3   much

much more beneficial it is to let out an estate
to farmers, for them to find the stock, cultivate the land, and employ the peasants, not
only in mere profit of the year, but with a
view to future improvements, which must
always be conducted with far more effect by
the people who work for their own interest,
than by others who do it for a master, and a
master perhaps who is always absent, or, if
present, who understands nothing of the matter. What great improvements have been
made in England by tenants, who enjoy the
benefit during their lease, and then pay a fresh
rent to their landlords on account of those
very improvements! In population also the
prince would reap a very great benefit; for
when men are working for themselves, their
industry will be very different from that of
servants; and in proportion to the general industry, must population be: the peasants
would likewise meet with less oppression, and
consequently increase more.

They sow a good deal of wheat in this line
of country; but their principal crop is barley.
I observed many plantations of hops in the
warm vales, where the soil is rich and deep:
it is a common culture in most parts of Bohemia, I am told; and when the spot chosen
for a hop-garden is suitable, they find it more
profitably

profitably applied than for any other crop.
Beer is a very great article of trade throughout
the kingdom, much being exported to all the
furrounding countries ; this makes barley and
hops particularly advantageous. Saffron is
another crop, which I faw now and then : they
prefer a light, dry loam on a ftratum of rock
for it ; they think it very profitable; an acre
of good faffron is worth about three pounds
here. Turneps and cabbages they have in
large quantities for the winter fupport of
their cattle : they prefer the latter in general:
I faw many crops fomewhat advanced in
growth, but they do not feem to be attentive
to keeping them free from weeds.

The 17th I reached Leutmyffel, at the diftance of forty-five miles, paffing through two
or three pretty towns upon the banks of the
Elbe. This country is more beautiful than
the preceding, and of a richer foil ; in fome
parts there are hills, but not fo great as to be
unprofitable land, while the vales form fome
very rich arable and meadow land; moft of
which is pretty well cultivated, under wheat,
barley, and beans, which are much fown
here: wheat yields from two, to two and an
half quarter per acre ; barley fomething more;
beans four quarters ; they choofe for thefe
their ftiffeft wet foils. They feed on their mea-

X 4   dow

dows large herds of cows and oxen; and keep
many sheep, but do not manufacture the
wool; most of it is sold to Silesia and Saxony,
both of which are much more industrious
countries: They work up however some of
their own flax into the same sort of linnens, as
are made in Silesia, which is an employment
of the poor people in many of the little
towns in this kingdom; their earnings at this
work are very small; a weaver in Silesia will
earn about three and sixpence a week; but
in Bohemia not more than half a crown: But
provisions of all sorts are very cheap in both
these countries. I saw two or three country
seats belonging to noblemen; they are all
built in the castle form, with a moat round,
and seem to be extremely spacious; a nobleman of great fortune in this country, has sel-
dom less than two or three hundred servants
about him, when at his castle in the country;
and he is an absolute monarch upon his estate,
with power over every thing but life and
death, and the royal revenue officers. This
kind of dominion over all the lower classes,
flatters the vanity and pride of the great, more
than the amount of the advantages they would
gain by the peasants being free; it is like the
contrast of absolute authority to the limited
power possessed by some kings; the latter
makes

makes their people happy and rich, and might
have the fame effect upon themfelves, but
they are all hunting after the former.

The 18th I got to Olmutz, the capital of
Moravia, the diftance forty miles; croffing the
mountains which feparate the two countries,
thefe are not very lofty, nor craggy, but they
fill a track of country, of feveral miles broad;
they exhibit a wild territory, but little of
which is cultivated: The peafants that inhabit thefe hills, are a rough intractable fet
of men, that will not fubmit to the oppref-
fiions under which their brethren of the plains
groan; they have been often in rebellion, not
againft the fovereign, but the lords to whom
they are vaffals; they are in many refpects
treated much better; and their houfes and
little farms make a much better appearance;
they have more and better cattle; fome of
them are in poffeffion of fmall pieces of land
which they have purchafed, and all are extremely tenacious of this kind of property;
they do not work for their mafters more than
three days in a week. It is always to be remarked, that the gradations of freedom are
ever to be found in mountainous countries; in
general fuch are free; but even under abfolute monarchs they enjoy more liberty, than
the fubjects of the fame prince who inhabit
                                        plain

plain countries: To live in hilly countries, requires more activity and vigour of body; the very moving from one place to another is laborious, the cold and bluftering climates found in them, contribute to bracing up the human body, and to make it hardy. It is the fame effect as is feen in cold climates, compared with hot ones, in whatever parts of the world they may be found. After the mountains are paffed that feparate the two countries, I went through a great extent of foreft, and marfh land, very little of which is cultivated; and not much of it would pay for culture, unlefs the country in general was richer than it is.

Olmutz is a fmall but very well built city, prettily fituated on the little river Moravia. It is a ftrong place both by nature and art: fo that the King of Pruffia, when he made the famous irruption into Moravia, and laid fiege to it, did not feem to have had good intelligence of the ftate of the town, or the garrifon. The ftreets are regular and well paved, and there are many good houfes in it; the only publick buildings of any note, are the Jefuits college, the bifhop's palace, and the townhoufe; the market place is furrounded by feveral well built houfes. It is an agreeable town, and the inhabitants feem to be a very fociable
people,

people, with more activity and induſtry, than
is to be found among the Bohemians. Pro-
viſions are very cheap here: I lived at the
Empreſs's Arms inn, two days, upon exceeding good fiſh and fowl, and good Hunga-
rian wine, and when I paid my reckoning, I
found that ſix ſhillings went to the full, as far
as a guinea in England. Beef is only three
half pence a pound ; mutton is ſometimes ſold
at a penny; and a fat turkey is to be bought
for fourteen pence.

The 21ſt I left Olmutz, and proceeded to
Brinn, the diſtance thirty miles, through
a much more fertile country than north of
Olmutz ; it is better peopled, and much
more of it cultivated: They do not ſow much
wheat here, but a great deal of rye, barley,
peaſe, and beans ; and the crops in general,
carried a good appearance ; they keep great
herds of cattle, feeding them in winter on
cabbages, turneps, and ſtraw ; all the latter,
which they give to their cattle, they cut almoſt as ſmall as chaff, with an engine made
on purpoſe ; very different from the chaff-cut-
ter uſed in England. They chop the turneps,
or cabbages into ſmall pieces, and give them
with chopt ſtraw, and find that they go much
the farther, and nouriſh the cattle much better. I never heard of any thing of this ſort
being

being practifed in England; yet I fhould apprehend that it could not fail of anfwering
extremely; it is certainly much worth the
trial.   They have vaft herds of fwine, which
find their own fubfiftance in woods, and
fwampy grounds for moft part of the year.
They fatten them on beans, peafe, and potatoes, which they cultivate on purpofe: felling great quantities of bacon to Vienna, &c.

Brinn is well fituated on the confluence of
two rivers, and is reckoned the ftrongeft place
in Moravia; it has a caftle that is very ftrong;
the Auftrians have ufually a good garrifon
here; feveral new fortifications have been added both to this place, and to Olmutz fince
the laft war, which I fuppofe were occafioned
by the King of Pruffia's bold march into this
country, which alarmed them exceffively at
Vienna.   There are about fix thoufand inhabitants in Brinn; the ftreets are narrow and
crooked, but many of the houfes very well
built, and fome of the publick edifices make
a tolerable appearance, particularly the Jefuits
college, and the churches of St. James, and
St. Thomas.

The 22d I reached Laba, a little town
thirty miles from Brinn; the country between
them is better than the preceding; has lefs
wafte land, fewer forefts and marfhes; and
the

the arable land beyond comparifon better cultivated. This is in a great meafure owing to
the attention given to hufbandry-improve-
ments by the court of Vienna. They were
at the expence fome years ago, of bringing feveral Flemifh farmers from the country, between Oftend and Bruges; three of them were
fettled in this country, being fupplied with all
forts of implements, cattle, houfes, land,
&c. by the Emprefs Queen, and fixed upon
fome wafte, but very fertile lands belonging
to the crown. They have had a large fuccef-
fion of Moravian peafants, regularly working under them, in order to be inftructed in
the Flemifh hufbandry; who being difcharged
when frefh ones are taken, have much fpread
feveral excellent cuftoms, and will in all probability, much improve the agriculture of the
greateft part of the province. The effect has
already been very confiderable; for though
thefe Flemings do not occupy a thoufand
acres of land in all, yet their methods already
fpread over a country near fifteen miles long;
all the hufbandry of which is by their means
much improved. They have introduced clover here, which turns out one of the moft
beneficial crops that can be fown; they have
alfo made this culture of clover a preparation
for wheat, fo that they have almoft entirely
banifhed

banifhed the cuftom of fallowing for wheat,
which was the common method in Moravia.
Spurry they alfo brought with them, with
which they feed cows. To them likewife the
Moravians are indebted for a much more fy-
ftematic management of manure, than what
they formerly followed : They form compofts
of dung, rotten vegetables, vaft quantities of
leaves, fwept up on purpofe in the open
forefts, turf, afhes, and other materials, which
they mix together feveral times, and fpread
upon their clover fields—and on their cabbage
grounds : They have alfo made them abundantly more attentive in keeping all their crops
clear from weeds and in good order, by hoeing and weeding ; all the cabbages I faw in
this diftrict, which has been profited thus
from the example of the Flemings, were in
very fine order, both in refpect to pulverized
foil, and a clearnefs from weeds.

I faw the caftle of baron Skulitz, who had
been extremely attentive in fpreading this
good Flemifh hufbandry. He refides conftantly on his eftate, and makes agriculture
not only his bufinefs, but alfo his amufement :
Immediately on their exhibiting a culture, fuperior to the old management of the Moravians, he followed it with fo much intelligence and fpirit, that he has advanced the value

lue of his estate considerably : He entered
presently into all their views, and introduced
the best husbandry of the Austrian provinces
upon his own lands. Falling into discourse
on the road with one of his bailiffs, he pointed out to me several large tracks of land,
which not long ago were entirely waste, but
are now by this worthy nobleman's attention, better cultivated than most of the province. He has introduced various new branches of husbandry, which answer better than
common crops; among these, hops and saffron he brought from Bohemia; madder from
Silesia; and he raises both hemp and flax in
large quantities : All these crops he is remarkably attentive to, and gives them such
uncommon fair play, that his first trials, contrary to what is generally met with, turned
out greatly successful, from whence he has
been induced to continue them ever since, and
greatly to enlarge all his plantations of them,
by which, and various other means, he has
improved his revenues in a surprizing manner.

The owners of extensive landed estates, in
poor countries, have all such an opportunity
of increasing their income ; and it is very
amazing they do not oftener take advantage of
it. If, like the nobleman here mentioned,

I

they

they would refide upon their eftates, inftead
of fpending all their time in the capital,
fquandering their revenues in a gulf of luxury,
the meafure of which is never full, and
which cannot fail of impoverifhing them, and
bringing them into the moft flavifh depen-
dence upon the will of the court; if they
would act thus, they would find money flow
into their coffers in a far greater abundance
than they can ever hope to receive from the
fmiles of minifters; at the fame time that
they would refide where a fhilling goes as far
as a pound. In the profufion of a capital, the
greateft eftates are fpent without making any
unufual figure; but in the country, half the
income would enable them to build and furnifh coftly palaces, and raife whole cities
around them to be witneffes of their fplendor.
—I have, in the courfe of my travels, met
with feveral inftances, which fhew, in the
cleareft light, the enjoyment and undoubted
happinefs which this kind of life confers,
even upon noblemen, whofe rank and revenue
would allow them all the amufements of any
metropolis. It is a moft happy thing to any
country, when a fovereign gives all the encouragement in his power to promote this
rural attention in nobles, which cannot fail
of

óf turning out highly beneficial to the whole community.

The 23d I got to Vienna, which is five-and-twenty miles from Laba, through a country that is very unequal, part of it being very rich, populous, and well cultivated, and much of it hilly, wild, and to appearance barren. In the cultivated tracks are many noblemen's feats ; and the hufbandry around them is vifibly much better than elfewhere, which is owing to their drawing the peafants, as it were, into a ftring around them. They plant great quantities of faffron, which they reckon the moft profitable crop they have : they have alfo plenty of good crops of wheat and barley ; and their extenfive meadows and paftures feed large herds of cattle, which from the neighbourhood of Vienna turn to very good account. I faw feveral crops of the turnep cabbage for cattle. But hufbandry fuffers much in all this country, and indeed through moft parts of Germany, for want of inclofures : they might eafily make them, and at a fmall expence, but neglect the work entirely, which muft be for want of fully underftanding the advantages of them : Indeed, labour is of fo little value, that every fort of cattle has always a keeper with them, tho'

Vol. III.   Y   the

the herd is ever fo fmall, yet corn and faffron often fuffer.

Vienna is fituated on the fouth fide of the Danube, but has not the advantage of that great river running through it; for it ftands on a fmall branch of it, there being feveral iflands formed here, by the river dividing it-felf. If the fuburbs are included, it is a very large city, but within the walls and fortifica-tions it is only three miles in circumference. It is regularly fortified, but has fo few out-works, as to be a place of fmall ftrength, and only defended by a fmall army. At the fiege in 1683, the Turks fhewed themfelves to be extremely ignorant in the art of conduct-ing fuch an enterprize; and their engineers were miferable ones, elfe they might have taken the city fome time before the King of Poland raifed the fiege; and had that event happened, Hungary had now been in poffef-fion of the Ottomans.

Vienna within the walls makes a moft ine-legant appearance, from the narrownefs of the ftreets. I am one who would not give fix-pence for a fine building, if there is not a fufficient area to view it from. The Englifh boaft of the church of St. Paul's at London; and will fometimes affert it equal to St. Peter's at Rome; but if it were doubly finer, I fhould
prefer

prefer St Peter's, from the opportunity one has of viewing it; and the area around a great building, ought to be so much esteemed a part of it, as to be criticised with it ; and the architect's abilities called in question for faults in it, as much as if he blundered in the proportion of the cupola. Thus in Vienna, there are many palaces (of which I had read and heard much,) in streets as narrow as old Bristol; and at the same time all the houses are five, six, seven, and some of them eight stories high ; and it is said, they have almost as many stories of cellars under ground, as of floors above. Formerly all the windows were grated with iron bars like prisons, from the street to the upper floor, and vast numbers of houses are so now, but I see it is left off in the principal palaces.

The imperial palace is a structure that will answer to none that sees it; it consists of several courts, surrounded with irregular buildings; though, notwithstanding some late additions, it makes but a very mean appearance; the apartments are neither spacious, nor furnished in the manner one would expect, for a court long famed as one of the most expensive in Europe. The library is supposed to rank among the first in Europe; the number of

volumes

volumes are not less than ninety thousand; and the collection of manuscripts, supposed to be extremely valuable. I was shewn several great curiosities, but upon these occasions there never is time allowed for any useful examination, and if there were, it would signify little to the unlearned in the oriental tongues, in which the most valuable manuscripts are written.

Many of the palaces of the nobility, are most magnificent structures; that of the great Eugene with his famous library and collections I had most pleasure in viewing; the Mansfield palace, and that of count Daun, are also great edifices, with several others, in which the painting, gilding; carving, and furniture are as rich as possible.

The university of Vienna, is very famous in Germany and Hungary; the number of students is considerable, and they have good accommodations for those of fortune, and many valuable privileges.

There is not much worth seeing in the churches of Vienna; the cathedral is the principal, and it is a large building; but nothing is uncommon in it but the heighth of its spire, which, since Strasburg, is become French, is the highest in the empire. The Jesuits church is a fine building; and the convents of Carmelites,

Carmelites, Francifcans, Benedictines, and Auftin Friars, are vifited by thofe who take any delight in viewing thefe fort of buildings; for my part, I have an averfion at feeing fuch ufelefs edifices filled with tribes of pernicious orders of lazy priefts, who do nothing to gain their livelihood, but are maintained by the induftry of every body elfe: It is amazing, that Roman catholick princes do not find out that every monk in their dominions might be a foldier, without the country fuffering a whit the more: and in many cafes the foldier would pay well for his maintenance; but as to the monk, he is fubfifted in the moft unufeful of all fpecies of idlenefs.—But there are other inftances of the catholick piety of Vienna, befides her monks and nuns; in one of the fquares, is a very large and coftly ftatue of the Trinity, reprefenting the Deity clafping Chrift in his arms, and the Holy Ghoft hovering over them. This was erected by the Emperor Leopold, inftead of an equeftrian ftatue, which in other cities would have been erected to the fovereign. To this famous piece of folly, all the Roman catholicks bow as they pafs. Religious prejudices fhould certainly be laid afide by all travellers; but is it poffible for a man of fenfe not to rejoice, that education has not enflaved him to

Y 3

an

an obfervance of, or veneration for fuch mum-
mery? In many inftances, religion makes Roman catholick countries extremely difagreeable to travel through.

I brought feveral letters of recommendation
to Vienna, to perfons from whofe converfation, I expected fome valuable information
concerning the general ftate of all the Auftrian dominions at prefent, in refpect of a-
griculture, manufactures, commerce, revenues, and military power ; but I was ftrangely
difappointed : there is a haughty referve in
every man of the leaft confequence here,
which not only precludes any information of
this fort ; but at the fame time renders a refidence in any but a publick character very difagreeable at Vienna. But after all my letters
had failed, that is, introduced me only to
people who thought that I had no bufinefs
with any thing but eating, drinking, going
to court, and playing at cards, a life by no
means agreeable to me ; after this I fell acci-
dentally into company with a field-officer in
their fervice, a native of Milan : this gentleman was extremely communicative, very fenfible, and had travelled often through moft of
the dominions of the Emprefs Queen. He
gave me a very rational, and candid account
of things, as appeared by his manner, and
the

the confirmations I had afterwards from
feveral perfons in other parts of Europe.   To
agriculture this gentleman had not at all attended; he could give me no more account
of its general ftate in the countries he had been
in, than with that of the moon. I found
from him however, that the manufactures
which have lately been eftablifhed in Hungary, flourifh very much; the Emprefs Queen,
and her minifters, have long been eager to
cloath her troops with her fubjects manufactures; inftead of felling all their wool unma-
nufactured.   Hungary, as well as Auftria,
Bohemia, and Moravia, feed many fheep,
efpecially Hungary, a great part of which is
a continued and fertile fheep-walk. Great
numbers of Hungarians have been fet to
work upon this wool; and weavers, fpin-
ners, reelers, &c. brought from Flanders,
to teach the natives to work it ; and many of
them have proved very docile in learning : fo
that at prefent, woollen goods are made to the
amount of near an hundred thoufand pounds
a year, which is a very great thing in Hungary—where, before thefe exertions, were
no manufactures at all—They are eftablifhed
in moft of the populous towns of that kingdom; and if they are brought, to employ the
poor people in them, who have no other em-

Y 4   ployment,

ployment, it will be an immenfe acquifition, and fave the export of very great fums of money. As to trade, the inland fituation of the Auftrian dominions, is fuch as allows of very little foreign commerce. Attempts were made at Trieft, but they were fo languid, and fuffered fuch interruptions during the war, that the commerce of the port is yet nothing that deferves mention; notwithftanding that an active prince, liberal in ufeful expence, and attentive to fuch improvements, might have made Trieft the feat of a confiderable commerce; but all thefe circumftances have been wanting.

The revenues of the dominions of the houfe of Auftria, are confiderable; the following account of them was given to this gentleman, by a perfon who had many opportunities of being well informed.

Bohemia	£ 700,000
Moravia	190,000
Hungary	400,000
Auftria	400,000
Tranfilvania	50,000
Sclavonia and Croatia	100,000
Stria, Curinthia, and Carniola	200,000
Tyroll, Brixen, Trent	160,000
The countries of Swabia	20,000

The

The Netherlands ———— 150,000
Milan, and Mantua ·——— 400,000
Tuscany ——— ———— 500,000

Total ——— ——— £ 3,270,000

What degree of accuracy there is in this table; I am not able to ascertain, but from the information I have received from other hands, I believe the total to be near the truth: but Tuscany must not be reckoned : the common idea at Vienna coincides with these particulars; which makes the Imperial revenue near three millions : though there are some sanguine politicians, who insist on it's amounting to five; but that is much exaggerated. The revenues of all these countries might be very much improved; nobody doubts but a better system of taxation, and a more œconomical collection would raise five millions, with very near as much ease to the people as three at present; but the lower classes of the people throughout most of these dominions are miserably fleeced, and pillaged, while the nobility escape with paying a much less proportion than they ought. The Netherlands might in particular yield a very considerable revenue, and prove the finest and most profitable provinces

vinces belonging to the houfe of Auftria; but
in order to that, great changes fhould be made
in the conftitutions of the cities ; manufactures fhould receive encouragement, and commerce be re-eftablifhed in the ports; all which
might be eafily done, and the revenues of the
fovereign become wonderfully improved;
whereas at prefent they yield no more
than might be expected if they were fituated no better than Auftria, or Moravia,
inftead of being the fineft fpot in Europe, in
every refpect; and inhabited by a people naturally as induftrious as any in the world.
Flanders, fince the Dutch were mafters of the
navigation of Antwerp has wanted a port ;
but Oftend, for an hundred thoufand pounds,
might be made as good a one as any in Europe
for merchantmen.

The many improvements, which have been
talked of by the court of Vienna for the hereditary dominions, in agriculture, manufactures,
and commerce, were they put in execution,
would at the fame time much improve the revenue, and in a manner free the country of
thofe evils, which ufually flow from increafing the publick income of a crown. But
there is a dilatorinefs and a languor in every
thing tranfacted at this court, even in its own
moft intricate concerns, that damp the fpirit

of

of all improvement, fo that any object of this
fort, upon a moderate computation, will be
talked of half a century, before it is executed;
this was the cafe with the eftablifhment of
the woollen manufacture in Hungary, and with
every thing elfe: fo that it is not thought the
Auftrian revenues, however they would admit
of it, will for a long time be put upon a better
footing than they are, or have any other improvements than what refults from oppreffing
the lower claffes of the people ftill more : than
which no meafure can give a greater ftab to
all general national improvements. Was the
King of Pruffia poffeffed of the Auftrian dominions in exchange for his own, we fhould
foon fee them make a very different appearance ; he would raife much greater revenues,
with far greater eafe to the people; and would
throw fuch a vigour into all the tranfactions
which the poffeffion of Flanders, and the Italian dominions would introduce him to, that
the importance of them would fpeedily appear
in a very different light from what they do at
prefent.

The great object of attention at Vienna, is
the army; this is fo far reprehenfible in politicks, as it encreafes the neceffity of laying a
foundation previous to every fuperftructure : it
is the revenue that pays and fupports the army,
and

and all increafe of the latter muft depend on a foregoing increafe of the former: to raife a great revenue is much more effential, than to raife a great army; but the foldiers have a peculiar faculty of fwallowing up a revenue, they have none at creating it. That prince therefore, who would be truly formidable, fhould attend to the profperity of his income, before he thinks of greatly increafing his troops.

The following are the particulars of the prefent ftanding forces of the houfe of Auftria. I infert them on the fame authority as the above paper of the revenue; believing from other information which I have received, that it is near the truth; though I fhould remark, that all lifts of armies are apt to exceed the reality, rather than fall beneath it.

	Men.
Dragoons	23,846
Curiaffers	16,000
Huffars, and Croats	14,640
Hunters	6,300
Free troops	8,000
Infantry	164,386
Artillery	2,800
Total	235,972

The

The whole army, whatever the total may be, is certainly in excellent order ; the regiments full, and well officered, their cloathing regularly delivered, their arms much better than ever ; the artillery very numerous ; and no expence has been fpared in forming engineers ; the magazines of ammunition and all forts of military ftores, full, and in good order : thefe attentions have occupied the court ever fince the peace, and they have been indefatigable in them. Now, that all thefe particulars are compleated, they are employed in repairing all the fortifications in Bohemia, Moravia, Auftria, Hungary, and Tranfilvania ; new ones are in fome places erecting, and many old ones greatly improved ; this is a work of immenfe expence, and confequently it goes on flowly. In every one of thefe particulars, the Auftrians ftrength is greater than at the breaking out of the laft war. I before remarked, that the cafe was the fame with the King of Pruffia. Thefe potentates are certainly jealous of each other ; but I believe in no refpect that threatens a frefh war : but the ftate of affairs in other parts, makes it neceffary for them to be ftrongly armed. The afpect of affairs in Pruffia and Poland, fills the houfe of Auftria with uneafinefs ; and although Pruffia efpoufes in her manifeftos the fame caufe in Polifh affairs as

the

the Ruffian Emprefs, ftill it can only be, becaufe the power of that empire is too great for
him to break with. Moft certainly the increafe of the formidablenefs of Ruffia, ought
in good politicks to fill both Pruffia, and Auftria with the deepeft jealoufy; future alliances
with it, in cafe of a new war in Germany, muft
be very uncertain; and againft whoever fhe
declares, her weight will probably fall too
heavy to be refifted. The opportunity of the
war between the Ruffians and Turks, has generally been taken by the Auftrians for attacking the Porte: fuch a meafure now would
infure the reftoration of Belgrade and Servia,
and perhaps yet greater advantages; but
not making ufe of it, may be owing to two
reafons: firft, in return for the Turks not
playing the fame game when the Emprefs
Queen was at war with Pruffia; and fecondly,
becaufe fuch a conduct would give greater advantages to the arms of Ruffia, than the houfe
of Auftria wifhes to fee.

C H A P-

C H A P T E R   X.

Journey from Vienna through Auſtria—Deſcrip-
tion of the Archdutchy—Bavaria—Munich—
Revenues and forces.—

JULY 1ſt, I left Vienna, and that day travelled forty miles to St. Poltu, through a
very various country. Near Vienna, it is very
gay, being lightly adorned with villas, which
have extenſive gardens, and planted groves
about them, but all in a miſerable taſte. I
ſtopped to view one pretty near the road, which
the poſtilions told me belonged to a great nobleman at court ; a deſcription of the ground
before the houſe will give a tolerable idea of
the taſte moſt prevalent here in ornamenting
their country ſeats. A canal with a ſmall
bridge over it in the center, parted the area
before the houſe from the road ; from the
bridge to the houſe door was about a hundred
yards ; a broad ſtone-way led from one to
the other ; on each ſide ranged in exact order
a ſtatue, an urn, and a croſs interchangeably ;
theſe were on a ſlip of graſs : on the other
ſide two canals nicely laid out, like the former,
by rule, and at each corner of the three, a
ſtatue. The ground on each ſide was formed

into

into a grafs-plot, furrounded by a parterre of flowers, and in the center of each plot, a fmall fountain. From thefe particulars of the approach to a rural villa, all unfeen may be very exactly guefled; and it evidently appears that the Auftrians are at leaft one hundred years behind us in the art of gardening. It is the fame with the French, and all the other nations of Europe. In fome gardens I was fhewn when in Italy, before I was told that they were executed in imitation of nature, upon the plan of my countryman Brown, whofe fame had reached there; and it is not eafy to be conceived how ridiculous every thing was; the leaft deviations from line and compafs work, amidft a great deal of it, were efteemed exertions in the art of imitating nature. A more ridiculous jumble was never feen; much worfe than thofe made purely artificial.

Ornamenting a piece of ground, in the manner of our great gardener, and in the tafte yet fuperior, in which fome private gentlemen in England have laid out their grounds, is an art that requires genius, and more attention than will ever be given to it, in countries where they refide ten months out of the twelve in the capital, and very many, the other two alfo: where this is the cafe, the expence will not be fpared, which we fee in every thing that re-

3   lates

lates to the country; no article about a nobleman while he refides in the country in England, but what infinitely exceeds the fame with
any foreign nobleman of equal fortune. Their
wealth is all expended upon their town houfes,
and their town refidence; it is not therefore to
be wondered at any more, that the Englifh
have not fuch fine palaces in London, as that
the French and Italians have not fuch fine
country feats.

Thefe forty miles do not exhibit an agriculture that is very flourifhing; yet the country is not much in want of people, for the
towns and villages are thick. The foil is in
general very good; but they do not feem to
have any ideas of cultivating it with neatnefs;
wild fhrubbery grounds are fuffered to break
into the corn, in ragged borders, and fmall
wafte fpots, where the plough, upon account
of fome hillock, or hole, does not go, are
left covered with weeds, to blow all over their
fallows; they have no idea of cleaning fuch
fpots by way of prevention, and fuch numbers
of them, as I faw in this day's journey, would
not be met with in half an Englifh county.
They fow large quantities of faffron, which
they reckon a profitable culture, an acre yielding a produce of about three pounds, if the
crop is good. There are many vineyards,

but the wine fells fo badly, that they affured me, corn and faffron ftand in general much better; and they do not confine their vines to tracks improper for ploughing.

Wheat, barley, rye, peafe and beans, are commonly cultivated, but no oats; the crops are but midling. Turneps, turnep cabbages, cabbages, and potatoes, are cultivated in large quantities; the former for cattle, and the potatoes for fattening hogs, for which they boil them. They have large herds of fwine, which feed all fummer long in the woods, many of which are extenfive. Horned cattle are alfo very plentiful here, and as they houfe them in the winter, they raife large quantities of dung, which ought to enfure a much better hufbandry than theirs. I paffed a fmall farm, near St. Poltu, that was cut out of a wafte, and to appearance a barren common, on the fide of a large hill; difpofed into ten fields by beautiful quick hedges, which put me in mind of the beft cultivated part of England: the inclofures rifing one above another, on the fide of the hill, were feen diftinctly from the road; they were covered with various crops, which appeared much fuperior to thofe of the cultivated parts of the country I had paffed; the houfe was fmall, but extremely neat. As foon as I had looked attentively at this very agreeable fight, I was going

ing

ing to make up to it; but recollecting that I
fhould be in the dark, I determined to go on to
the ftage, and come next morning to view that
farm, which feemed a creation in the midft of
a defart.

I accordingly put my intention in execution,
the morning of the 2d, and returned about
three miles to the place, and afking for the
mafter of it, he appeared immediately; a fine
tall open countenanced foldier, in an old fuit
of regimentals. I defired to fee his farm, upon which he very readily walked with me into
it. I went through all the ten inclofures; the
hedges were regularly planted, and had each of
them a ditch; the gates were all in good order, and every thing carried an appearance of
neatnefs, moft uncommon in Germany. He
had three meadows, each of them watered by
a fmall ftream he had brought from the hill
above his farm; it filled a little pond for wa-
tering the cattle, and might be conducted at
pleafure in the proper feafon, over all parts of
the fields for manuring them, which he prac-
tifes in winter and fpring. He had a field of
wheat, another of barley, two of clover, and
three of turneps and cabbages; and his fields
were all much of the fame fize, being each
about fix Englifh acres. Turneps and cabbages he grew on his fallow for cleaning the
                  Z 2   land;

land; succeeded them with barley, and then took clover, upon which he sows his wheat. This husbandry, which nearly resembles the best of Flanders, surprized me in the midst of Austria, where nothing of the kind is to be found. He keeps a dairy of cows; a small flock of sheep on the neighbouring waste, and oxen for ploughing and carting; he houses all his cattle in winter; his sheep every night in sheep houses; and litters every thing well with fern, which he cuts upon the waste. He is extremely attentive to raising large quantities of dung, which he manages by keeping as many cattle as he possibly can, and by mixing turf, and virgin earth with his dung as the cattle make it all winter long; by this means he is enabled to manure three fields, or eighteen acres very richly every year; but what gives a virtue to his dunghill, superior to any thing else is his bringing all the human ordure away from the little town of Poltu, for which, some of the inhabitants ignorant of its value, give a trifle for taking it away; he is at the expence of cleaning all the necessaries there, and of carting it to his farm; he mixes it up with his dung and virgin earth, and assures me that it forms the richest compost in the world; all the manure he raises in this manner, being applied to his turnep and cabbage grounds, he

gets

gets prodigious crops of thofe vegetables; and
I remarked that they were kept perfectly free
from weeds by hoeing: his cabbages are all
planted in regular rows on ridges, and the
fpaces between the rows ploughed feveral
times while growing, as well to kill the weeds
as to keep the land in good tillage, all which
appeared to me to be an excellent fyftem.
His crops of wheat yield four quarters an
acre; his barley five, his clover gives four tons
of hay at two mowings; and his turneps and
cabbages maintain a vaft flock: an acre of the
former he reckons fufficient to winter-feed two
oxen or cows; one of cabbages will winter
three or four; but the expences of them are
higher.   All thefe crops I fuppofe are equal
to the beft cultivated parts of England.

Upon returning to his houfe he gave me
his hiftory.   He was a corporal in a regiment
of foot, quartered, during fix years; in Flanders,
and Brabant, where, as he had always a ftrong
bent towards hufbandry, he remarked very
minutely their practices, and often worked in
the fields for Flemifh farmers.   Upon the war
breaking out with the king of Pruffia, he was
early in that fervice, and made a ferjeant, in
which capacity he behaved fo much to Mar-
fhal Daun's fatisfaction at the battle of Hock-
chirken, in fight of him, that he gave him pro-

Z 3   mifes

mifes upon the fpot, of promotion; but thefe
were not thought of afterwards, till being re-
prefented by another perfon to the Emprefs
Queen, and allowed by count Daun, fhe
perfonally afked him in the prefence of the
whole court, if he had any particular requeft
to make : upon which he afked his difcharge,
and a piece of this wafte to cultivate, being
born in the parifh. It was granted at once;
and further, his fovereign built him the
houfe and offices directly, and gave him an
hundred pounds to ftock the farm with.
With this fmall beginning he went to work
directly, and in nine years has raifed every
thing to the ftate I faw. His induftry is unbounded: though a continued fuccefs has attended all his undertakings, and his crops
prove as fine as poffible, bringing him in large
fums of money, yet he continues to work with
the fame feverity as ever, and does much the
greateft part of all the bufinefs of his farm with
his own hands; he has a fon about twenty-
five who executes the reft. The Emprefs has
been twice to fee him, and expreffed the higheft approbation of his conduct, and made him
a handfome prefent. His methods have been
put in execution under his own direction upon the eftates of two noblemen in the neighbourhood, and with good fuccefs; fo that this
worthy

worthy foldier is like to be of more benefit to his country than half a dozen generals; and fhews that nothing is of more importance than to eftablifh fuch examples as thefe in various parts of a dominion : for although they may fpread flowly, yet they certainly will fpread, and that they cannot do without being of very great public benefit.

By night, I reached a little town called Munf-bery, being half way to Lintz, at the diftance of thirty miles from Poltu, through a country that is cultivated in a very different manner from the foldier's farm I had left, whofe name (by the way) is Picco. The crops are in general bad and very full of weeds; and they feem to plough the foil very badly, although their ploughs are drawn by fix oxen, and they have two men, or a man and a lad to drive them, with another man to hold the plough; it is evident from this that the price of labour is low, or the farmer, that is the nobility, could not allow fuch a fuperfluity of hands; but while the time of the peafants belongs to their lords, without any pay, fuch inftances will be very common; but the whole fyftem makes a very different figure from my friend Picco's, whofe farm is a contraft to the whole arch-dutchy. They cultivate many hops, faffron, and vines, and thefe articles exhauft all their

Z 4   lands

lands applied to common hufbandry, of the
dung which they ought to have, without
yielding a return proportioned. Picco, when
I afked him why he did not cultivate thefe articles, affured me that none of them equalled
common crops in profit, provided the latter
were managed in the manner they ought to be;
and of this I have no doubt, for all thefe uncommon articles require a great deal of attention, and an infinity of labour, efpecially vines,
while the produce is of fuch a bad fort, that
the returns are inconfiderable. Near Lintz,
the country improves much, being in
itfelf finely variegated with hills and dales,
wood and water; it is alfo better cultivated;
there is a very little wafte land, and many feats
of the nobility are fcattered about it, attracted
I fuppofe by the agreeablenefs of the country.

Lintz is extremely well fituated on the
banks of the Danube : It is fmall, well built,
and a neat place; the ftreets well paved, and
kept very clean. What fets off the buildings
in an unufual manner, is the materials of
which they are raifed; being a white ftone
that preferves its colour. The market-place
is large and handfome; and is adorned with
two fountains. The Emprefs has a palace
here, well furnifhed, which from an high fituation over looks the courfe of the Danube very
beautifully;

beautifully; fhe ufed to come here often, but has not of late years. The Jefuits college is one of the beft buildings in the place, and the library has the reputation of being remarkably well chofen. This place is the capital of up-per Auftria; for the ftates affemble no where elfe. For its fize, it is very populous, which is owing to fome manufactures they have that are flourifhing; particularly that of woollen goods, and of filk and worfted; alfo gun-barrels, for which they are famous. The wool they work up is that of Auftria, and much comes from Bohemia; all thefe fabricks employ fix or feven hundred hands.

The 5th I got to Newberg in Bavaria, the diftance forty miles. This line of country is all very agreeable; from the inequalities of the ground, and its open groves, with many rivers; nor is it wanting in numerous little towns and villages, the neighbourhood of the Danube drawing many inhabitants, by the conftant trade carried on upon it; and by the numerous boats, barges, floops, &c. which pafs and repafs upon all forts of bufinefs. I obferved hops, faffron, and vines were com-mon culture, and fome flax, which is made into coarfe linnens in the neighbouring towns. Newberg is a little place, but very well built, and remarkably clean,. The Elector Palatine is fovereign of the dutchy, of which it is the capital;

capital and, has a fmall palace here, which however contains nothing worth feeing. The Jefuits church is the beft publick edifice in the place. The only trade of Newberg is wine; but very little of it is good; feveral forts are fold fo cheap as three halfpence a quart.

The 6th I reached Muldorf, the diftance fifty miles, through a very fine, populous, and well cultivated country, being part of the E-lectorate of Bavaria. There feems through this line of country, to be more induftry, ac-tivity and happinefs, than in any I had paffed for a long while, and yet the peafants are in a ftate of villainage as well as elfewhere, but they are treated in a kinder manner; have more property and better houfes; and many of them are alfo farmers, who by induftry and frugality have faved money; and find out the means of difpofing of it to good advantage. Much of this country is enclofed, than which there cannot be any improvement of fo much confequence; and the prefent Elector has given many privileges and encouragements to all who enclofe their farms, as well as exempting them from antient cuftoms and rights, which were extremely injurious to open lands. There are many vineyards in this country, and the wine is better than that of Auftria. Sheep feem to be a principal article in their hufband-ry; they keep great numbers, and of a better

4

breed

breed than common; which I am told was originally owing to procuring fome rams from Flanders. They yield large fleeces, and there are many manufactories for working up the wool, which receive great encouragement from the government. Every farm of any fize, (that is, every divifion of an eftate that is under a diftinct fteward or bailiff) has a large fheep houfe, with a roof, but open on one fide to the fouth; in this houfe they fold their fheep every night the whole year round, and depend on it principally for manuring their lands: when they begin to fold, they fpread over the floor light virgin foil, turf, fand, or peat earth, and fold upon it till it is very moift and dirty; then they make a frefh layer, and fo go on; but to every eighteen inches of depth, (for they remove the heap but once a year) they litter with ftraw ; and in extreme wet or fnowy weather they do the fame. This is upon the whole an excellent fyftem for raifing manure, and is a Flemifh cuftom, though with one or two variations : but I fhould think the fheep lying upon fuch a dunghill, would be prejudicial to their health; however, the Bavarians affert the contrary, and fay that the health of the animal does not fuffer in the leaft; and that the wool is much better than it would be if the fheep were expofed to the weather.

Muldorf

Muldorf is a little town, agreeably fituated, and regularly fortified, but it is not a place of any great ftrength; the ftreets are broad, ftrait, and well built, and the market-place fpacious, and furrounded with feveral buildings that are a great ornament to it. There are feveral churches and convents, but none that contain any thing remarkable.

The 7th I got to Munich, the diftance feven and thirty miles, and the country agreeable and well cultivated; there are many more nobility who refide conftantly on their lands in this country, than in any I have feen in Germany; and to this I attribute the advantage of the fuperior cultivation : for as the nobles are the farmers, it is no wonder that eftates there are managed better under the mafter's eye, than in his abfence. Although there are not many of them that are proficients in agriculture, yet a life paffed in the midft of its bufinefs, muft yield a greater knowledge of its circumftances than one which is entirely employed in the parade of a court. Befides, there can be little doubt but the nobles themfelves treat their peafants better than the race of bailiffs, agents, &c. who ufually opprefs and fqueeze them the more, in order to have the better opportunity of enriching themfelves; and I find it evident, wherever I have been in Germany, that the landlords are the richeft, and

and their eftates the beft cultivated, where the peafants are allowed fome degree of liberty and property. The happier that race of people, the better for the nobles; the latter will not in all cafes be brought to believe this, but nothing admits of clearer proof.

Their corn through this track of country looked very well; and I obferved particularly, that their fallows intended for next year were well ploughed, and clean; whereas they are full of weeds in many parts of Germany, and much fuch bad management as I had feen in Auftria. The foil here is a rich loam, with fome light tracks : they plough chiefly with oxen. They fallow their lands for wheat; and then fow barley; after the barley, they take peafe or buck-wheat, and then turneps, or cabbages; but they do not fow any clover, which the Auftrian foldier, and all Flanders and Brabant find fo profitable. Wheat yields two quarters and an half per acre, barley three, and buck-wheat four; and their turneps and cabbages are applied to feeding their cattle and fheep; but all are houfed in winter.

Munich I think without exception, the fineft city in Germany; Drefden, while in its grandeur, I am told furpaffed it; and fome parts of Berlin are very beautiful, and al things confidered, they now yield to this place. It is fi tuated on the river Ifer; which dividing

into

into several channels, waters all parts of the town: so that little streams run through many of the streets, confined in stone channels, which has a most clean and agreeable effect. The streets, squares, and courts are spacious, and airy; which sets off all the buildings much, and makes them appear finer than others much more costly in other cities. The streets in particular, are so strait, that many of them intersect each other at right-angles, and are very broad, and extremely well built. There are sixteen churches and monasteries in it, many of them very handsome edifices; these with the electoral palace, and other publick ings, take up near half the city: so that it may easily be supposed the place is in general very well built.

The principal of all these publick edifices, is the electoral palace, which is rather a convenient than an elegant building. It is very large; having four courts in it, and all of them large, but there is a want of finishing in the insides of all the places in Germany, that cannot fail disgusting an Englishman, who has been used to see the houses of the nobility in his own country finished to the garrets, as compleatly as a snuff-box; and certainly it is a most agreeable circumstance. In the palace of Munich, the finest room, which is the grand hall, being an hundred and eighteen feet

long

long by fifty two broad, is open to the roof,
fo as entirely to deftroy the effect which would
refult from fuch a fize if finifhed : birds fly
about in it as in a barn, and drop their fa-
vours on the heads of the company as they
pafs. I have in Germany feen many inftances
of unfinifhing equal to this. There is a great
profufion of marble in the feveral apartments,
but it is not wrought in an agreeable manner.
The furniture is in general old ; it has been
very rich, but has nothing in it ftriking ; nor
is the collection of pictures comparable to
many others in Germany. The Mufeum is
well filled with many curiofities ; of which
as Keyfler gives a lift, I fhall therefore fay no
more of them.—The Jefuits college is among
the fineft buildings belonging to the church :
it is very fpacious. The great church, and
the Francifcans monaftery, are alfo worth feeing ; the latter order is poffeffed of very great
revenues. Several palaces of the nobility make
a very good figure, and the town-houfe is
better than many I have feen. The number
of inhabitants is computed at fifty thoufand.

The palaces moft worth feeing are the E-
lector's country ones of Sleifheim and Nymphenburg, near Munich. Sleifheim is a fine
building, and much better finifhed than that
of Munich ; the portico fupported by marble
pillars is fine ; in the apartments, which are
                                    furnifhed

furniſhed in an agreeable manner, is a very
good collection of pictures, but they are
chiefly by Flemiſh maſters. Nymphenburg
exhibits the German taſte of gardening in
perfection; the Bavarians holding them to be
the fineſt in the empire; the ſituation, wood,
and water would admit of ſomething beautiful, but here is nothing but the old-faſhioned
fountains, ſtatues, monſters, &c.

It is thought by moſt perſons at Munich,
as well as in other parts of Germany, the electorate of Bavaria has thoroughly recovered the
miſchiefs it ſuffered in the war of 1744, and
is now as rich and populous as ever. The
electoral revenues are reckoned to amount to
ſix hundred thouſand pounds a year, and are
improving: the ſtanding army conſiſts of
eleven thouſand foot, and three thouſand
horſe; but the Bavarians ſay, their prince
could bring forty thouſand men into the
field; however, it is certain that, if he could
bring them there he could not maintain them,
without their being in the pay of foreigners.
While the houſe of Bavaria continues on good
terms with that of Auſtria, there is no danger
of its ſuffering by the electorate being again
made the ſeat of war.

F I N I S.